THE THINKER'S GUIDE TO

Evil

PETER VARDY & JULIE ARLISS

BOOKS

MediaCom
Education Inc.

Dedication

To Camilla and Isabelle

Copyright © 2003 John Hunt Publishing Ltd
46A West Street, Alresford, Hants SO24 9AU, U.K.
Tel: +44 (0) 1962 736880 Fax: +44 (0) 1962 736881

E-mail: office@johnhunt-publishing.com

www.o-books.net

Text: © 2003 Peter Vardy and Julie Arliss

Designed by Andrew Milne Design

Co-publishers for Australia and New Zealand are:
MediaCom Education Inc, PO Box 610, UNLEY 5061, SOUTH AUSTRALIA
www.mediacom.org.uk

To order and for further information on *The Thinkers Guide to Evil*

Telephone Australia: 1 800 811 311
New Zealand: 0800 833 477
Email: admin@mediacom.org.au

ISBN 1 903816 33 5

Reprinted 2004

A CIP catalogue record for this book is available from the British Library.

Printed by Ajanta offset & Packagings Ltd.

Cover illustration: Satan smiting Job with boils by William Blake

Inside Cover illustration: From Pilgrims Progress by Frank C Pape

CONTENTS

CHAPTER ONE

WHAT IS EVIL?

"The progress of the sciences has been colossal ... but from the spiritual point of view, we live in the lowest period of civilization. A divorce has come about between physics and metaphysics. We are living through an almost monstrous progress of specialization, without any synthesis." (Salvador Dali)

WHO IS EVIL?

Evil is one of the deepest and most central problems of human existence - a problem that every individual and every age must face for itself. This book will chart some of the options, will explore the alternatives and finally will leave the decision as to how to regard evil for you, the reader.

Hitler was generous and loyal. He loved children and supported friends when they were in difficulties. He had a great pride in the achievements of the German nation and a fierce intolerance of communism. Ethically he was in some ways ahead of his time, he was a vegetarian and a non-smoker. Hundreds of thousands of Germans, young and old, went to meetings where Hitler was speaking, he was a dynamic and charismatic man with a powerful and attractive personality. Clubs had pictures of him on their walls, men wanted to be like him and girls wanted to be near him. His physical presence seemed to express all that was best about Germany. He had the power to move people and to generate devotion in his followers. Hardly anyone within Germany spoke against Hitler. His sole aim was to create a better Germany. It was Hitler who first arranged the production of the Volkswagen – the "people's car". His aim was that every ordinary German family should be able to afford a car – and this was at a time when in every other country cars were the preserve of the wealthy. He aimed to restore dignity to the German people after they lost the First World War. The governments of France and Britain wanted to crush Germany but Hitler restored the German economy and renewed the German sense of pride by commissioning architects to built new buildings on a grand scale. He had a real sense of the beauty of certain types of German music and encour-aged young German boys and girls to enjoy healthy, outdoor past-times including walk-

Adolf Hitler

ing, sailing, mountain climbing and even gliding. Yet Hitler is now almost uni-versally regarded as one of the most evil and dangerous men who ever lived. His achievements included sending to death millions of German people whom he considered to be sub-human. This included very many German Jews.

The same can be said for other figures who have been held to have been evil. Stalin who, without remorse or pity killed millions of his people was a won-derful, loving grandfather. The leaders of apartheid South Africa institution-alized racism and made people with black skin second class citizens in their own country (they could not live in the cities, sit on park benches, travel on the same buses, use the same lifts, go to the same hospitals, eat in the same restaurants still less "go out with" or marry a "white" South African). Yet the care for family amongst the Afrikaner leadership, their pride in the country they had built against all the odds and, as they saw it, their Christian com-mitment was exceptional. South Africa in the apartheid years stood out as a beacon amongst other African countries with better education, better health care (for black as well as white people), better roads, a stronger economy and a fairer legal system than almost any other country in sub-Saharan Africa.

Neither Hitler nor Stalin, nor the apartheid leaders, would have regarded themselves as evil – although they might all have admitted that they had had to do some unpleasant things in order to achieve real change in the living conditions of their people. They would have been unlikely to admit that they as individuals were evil or that the things they did were evil.

Similarly most of us would accept that we have done unpleasant things, but few of us would accept that we have done anything evil – still less that we are evil. What, then, is evil? The Roman Catholic Church condemns artificial birth control and sex before marriage as intrinsically evil acts (that is they are evil in themselves) but even Roman Catholics who use artificial birth control and have sexual relationships before marriage, though they might consider that they had done something wrong, would not consider these to be **evil** acts.

Darth Vader from the film Star Wars.

SO, WHAT IS EVIL? Modern films often focus on the reality of evil and people have no difficulty in recognizing evil when they see it in these productions. The shelves of video stores are full of horror films often featuring vampires, devils and the like but the most popular films of all also deal with the reality of evil. For instance:

THE STAR WARS SERIES The classic science fiction series is a story of the struggle between good and evil. There is a mysterious "Force" running through the Universe which can be tapped by those who are able to do so – the Force has two sides, a dark side and a good side, and both sides are available to individuals who can "let the Force flow through them". Individuals can train and develop in their ability to use this force and the "Jedi knights" are the supreme exemplars. They have to undergo long and hard training – most Jedis use the good side of the Force but some turn to the Dark Side. There is an evil emperor who succeeds in turning one of the strongest and best Jedi Knights into his most loyal servant – Darth Vader. The power of the evil emperor and the dark side of the Force grows, and the viewer is left in no doubt that they would use any means to achieve the ends they seek. The dark side is challenged by a band of good friends who themselves have to make hard choices. They can choose to be instruments of the good side of the Force or they can choose to place self at the centre. In this series of films the existence of evil, represented by the emperor and Darth Vader, is unquestioned. The viewer is easily able to identify it because the "baddies" wear dark outfits and there is appropriate music played when the dark side is active. Evil in the world is never so easily identified but the solution to evil in the film is achieved by personal integrity, courage, the power of friendship and love.

Perhaps the appeal of the Star Wars films, (special effects apart), lies in the very real experience people have of evil and the challenge this makes upon individuals to fight it against the odds.

HANNIBAL LECTAR IN *THE SILENCE OF THE LAMBS* In the book and film, Hannibal Lecter eats people for pleasure. He would cut out their tongues or liver and serve these with a good Chianti and some beans. He is portrayed as incredibly dangerous – so much so that, before his escape, he had to be locked into a special suit made of steel and covered in chains whenever he was moved. Many consider him to be mad, but he is highly intelligent, thoughtful, and reflective and knows exactly what he is doing. He kills knowingly, thoughtfully yet in a terrible manner, which shows no trace of human warmth or concern. However when the agent who was chasing him, Clarice Starling, was in danger he cut off his own hand rather than hurt her because his sense of honour bound him to her by a debt of loyalty and something close to love. Hannibal Lectar challenges the reader to see that evil in the world is not two-dimensional. He is undoubtedly presented as an evil character, but people are rarely 100% evil – even the cannibal, Hannibal Lectar, reveals glimpses of courage, self-sacrifice and almost love.

HARRY POTTER Harry Potter is a young orphan growing up in a family that dislikes him. He lives in a cupboard under the stairs and is badly treated. However he learns when he is 11 years old that his parents were wizards and that Lord Voldemort killed them when he was a baby. Lord Voldemort is the most evil wizard who has ever lived. He sought to destroy the Potter family and succeeded in killing Harry's mother and father. However he was defeated at the moment he tried to kill Harry and lost his power, becoming a pale shadow of his former self. The book does not make clear exactly why Lord Voldemort's power failed him at the crucial moment, but the power of Harry's mother's love was clearly decisive as she died protecting him. He had many supporters who, when he was defeated, quickly admitted the error of their ways and pretended to conform to the norms of their society. Lord Voldemort constantly sought to regain his old power and is gradually helped to do so by his former followers who would use any possible means to achieve their ends.

At Hogwarts, the boarding school for wizards attended by Harry Potter, there are four houses. One of these is the house to which most of the evil wizards belonged – it is called Slytherin and its sign is the snake. Slytherin pupils are said (by the talking hat which decided which house pupils should go into) to be willing to do anything to achieve their ends. A boy in Harry's year at Hogwarts is a young man of the same age as him called Malfoy. Malfoy's father, Draco, was one of Lord Voldemort's supporters and his son uses every means in his power to make fun of Harry and to make his life difficult. Both Harry and Malfoy have close loyal friends but Harry and his friends show tolerance, understanding and care for those outside their group, and stand against the power of the Dark Lord. Malfoy and his friends serve their own interests, try to make life inconvenient for others and like the idea of the Dark Lord regaining his power because they believe this will be in their interests.

The Harry Potter books are more than just the story of an orphaned boy who makes good, they present the classic struggle between good and evil. Evil constantly reasserts itself and is attractive to many – particularly those who seek power and influence for their own ends. Others would like to stand against it but are too weak – Quirrel, Ginny Weasley and Peter Pettigrew.

Evil, in *Harry Potter*, is identified with a selfish search for power over others and is opposed by those who may have power but will only use power for the good of others. Such people are motivated by compassion and gentleness. Dumbledore, Headmaster of Hogwarts School, is a supreme example of this – he can see through appearances, trusts people he knows are good, and runs the school with the quiet confidence of one who knows his own power. He is VERY powerful and the only wizard feared by the Dark Lord, but he uses his power to nurture others not to destroy or control them.

THE LORD OF THE RINGS In this series of books and films evil is identified with a "Dark Lord", Sauron, who seeks power for himself and is willing to use any means to achieve his ends. The key to the story is the "one ring". There are nineteen rings, but one ring rules the others. The "one ring" was lost in a battle and had been missing – with the result that the power of Sauron was seriously reduced. He wants to find it once more, as it is the key to total power. The ring has powers of its own and seeks out those who will use it for evil ends. The ring wants to go back to Sauron and almost every one who holds it comes under its power. The only way to avoid the complete devastation that Sauron has in mind is to destroy the ring. But whoever holds the ring comes under its control and will be unable to resist the temptation to join the evil forces of Sauron. The hero of the story is a very ordinary hobbit, Frodo Baggins, who precisely because of his ordinariness is the only one who can carry out the task. He has no wish for power, no selfishness that the ring can fasten onto. He sets out reluctantly, obeying the instructions of the wise wizard, Gandalf, to destroy the ring but throughout his long saga the forces of evil (and even the forces of good that have been corrupted by the ring) seek to kill him and to take possession of the ring for their own ends.

This is a story about the attractiveness of evil. Evil is presented as virtually irresistible even for the best of people. When the moment of choice is presented – the choice to take the power offered by the ring, only very few can avoid it. Most people find it easy to live good lives and avoid the power of evil until tempted by its attractiveness. Even some who oppose Sauron find themselves unable to resist the temptation of evil. Saruman is the leader of the great order of wizards but he becomes convinced that the only way forward is to join the dark path and seek the ring to build his own power. Boromir, a brave warrior, deludes himself by thinking that he can use the power of the ring for good ends. However the power of the ring corrupts, absolutely, and he ends up attacking Frodo the ring bearer. This is a story of how people can use reason to convince themselves that they can achieve good things by doing bad things. It is also about how, strangely, the force of evil can unite people. The various forces of good which, at times, have been suspicious of each other, are united by the growing power of Sauron and determine to destroy the ring. Evil can sometimes have a positive effect in bringing people together to oppose a common enemy.

The sources of evil and suffering are often complex and unclear.

In modern books and films such as these and in sagas and epics stretching back further than the ancient Greeks, the struggle against evil is set forth. It is easy to identify where the evil lies and although combating it may involve a life and death struggle, the "enemy" is at least easy to identify. However, evil in the real world is not always so easy to identify. Making a judgment is often very difficult and made more difficult because the media does not always present both sides when reporting news. Two examples will help to make this clearer

1. ISRAEL AND THE PALESTINIANS

After the suffering of the Jews in the Second World War (see chapter on the Final Solution for further discussion of this) it was decided that the Jewish people should have a homeland. Various countries of the world were considered as possible places where an area of land could be made available for Jewish people to settle if they wished. It was finally agreed that the State of Israel should be formed. Boundaries were identified in the region of Palestine and it was agreed that any Jew in the world who wished to go there could go. A Jew has come to be defined as someone with Jewish ancestry, not necessarily a practicing Jew. The Jewish people refused to accept any other part of the world as a homeland as they believed that God had promised the land of Israel to them. In the Hebrew Scriptures it records that God promised this land to their forefather Abraham. At one time in history the Jewish people did have control over the full extent of land outlined in the Genesis text. This was during the time of King David, and they look back to this time as a golden age when God's promise to them was fulfilled.

When the formation of the State of Israel was agreed the land that Jews were allowed to occupy was clearly stated. It was not the full extent of the land

The Dome on the rock, a shrine of central importance and holiness in Islam, is built on the Temple Mount where once the Jewish temple stood,

promised in the Hebrew Scriptures to Abraham. The reason for this was that this area of land was already lived in by Palestinians, who also needed a place to live. Ever since the formation of the State of Israel there has been fighting between Jews and Palestinians. The news is always reporting stories of new outbreaks of violence. Since the formation of the State of Israel millions of Jews have gone to Israel, mostly from Eastern Europe, and the geographical limits agreed for their occupation have not been kept to. Israelis have started to live in areas that were given to Palestinians to live in. The majority of the Israeli people want certain key sites, and aim to take control over the whole region.

The Palestinians have their own perspective on this. The formation of the State of Israel resulted in the displacement of hundreds of thousands of Palestinians. Opinions differ as to why the Palestinians left. Many Israelis say that they left freely, whilst most Palestinians would say that they were driven out by terror tactics and great fear. Many Palestinian Arabs felt anger and resentment at being forced to leave their homes, olive groves, vineyards and lands. They were forced into refugee camps in the thin Gaza strip and many had no jobs and no running water. The Palestinian Arabs would ask why the Jews had the right to live in their country. The suffering of Jews during the holocaust was very great indeed and a homeland was a way of compensating the Jewish people for the terrible way they had been treated in Europe, but why Palestine? Palestinian Arabs do not accept the authority of the Hebrew Scriptures, which say that God has given the land to the Jews by divine right. They are Muslims and have lived there for more than a thousand years. Even if it is accepted by the Palestinians that the Jews are to live there, why does nobody make the Jews stay in the territories that were originally agreed? The Arab states surrounding Israel (including Jordan, Syria and Egypt) bitterly opposed the creation of the State of Israel and in 1967 launched a war to bring, as they saw it, freedom to the Palestinian Arabs. However the Israeli army was brilliantly efficient and within seven days had taken huge amounts of territory from the neighboring Arab states – particularly Jerusalem, the West Bank, the Gaza strip and Sinai. Sinai was eventually returned following a peace treaty with Egypt but today Israel still occupies, in clear disobedience to United Nations resolutions, land it conquered in the 1967 war and continues to expand Jewish settlements in these occupied territories. Europe and the United States of America do not actively support the Palestinians in their demand for justice. The grandchildren of the original Palestinian Arabs have few options open to them. Israel's population is growing and everybody, including women, has to do national military service. The army and resources of Israel are far superior to the Palestinians and they feel that they are being crushed as Israel follows its expansion program. Terrorist activity, including the use of suicide bombers, is all they have left. It is an attempt to try to restore what they see as justice. In their communities they are treated as heroes – to the Israelis and to most Americans they are evil terrorist fighters.

Where does the evil lie in this very complicated real life situation? Where is the evil that needs to be conquered and what criteria can be used to identify it? It is FAR more complicated than the world of film and literature suggests.

2. SEPTEMBER 11TH, 2001 On September 11, 2001 two airliners were hijacked and flown into the "Twin Towers" in New York whilst another airliner was crashed into the Pentagon. A fourth airliner was hijacked but whilst the passengers overpowered the hijackers the plane then crashed. The Twin Towers contained the offices of many international trading organizations and were in many ways a symbol of capitalism. More than 3000 innocent people died and around the world people were appalled at the suffering that took place.

To the Western world, those responsible for this act, as well as those who planned it, were evil and wicked. They were cruel and heartless with no feelings at all for the victims or their families. The world watched news footage of people throwing themselves out of the buildings, with no hope of surviving the fall, rather than be burnt alive in the flames. Anyone who could do this to other human beings must be **evil.** The President of the United States, George Bush, talked of an **"axis of evil".** The news, as the Western world received it through their TVs, radios and newspapers, was that **evil terrorists** had attacked and killed **innocent American civilians.** Americans had been crushed to death, or burnt alive. They had just been going to work, minding their own business and had never hurt anyone in their lives. When America announced that it would punish the evildoers, as well as any nation on earth who knowingly hid them from justice, there were few who so much as raised an eyebrow. It appeared that evil was easy to identify.

However, not everyone thought this. To some people in Iraq, Pakistan, Iran, and Egypt; to some Palestinians and to some in other Muslim countries these so-called "evil terrorists" were **martyrs.** These brave men had given their lives for their beliefs. At last someone was making a stand against the **injustices of American "imperialism"**. Some of these people described the "terrorists" as **freedom fighters** who had stood up against American support of Israel and the injustice of the treatment of the Palestinians – in particular the failure of America to condemn Israel for ignoring United Nations resolutions and providing support for Israel by giving it huge amounts of money and the very latest weapons. Others saw it as a protest on behalf of devout Muslims against the whole way of life in the West. A protest against the way the West regards sex and money, the way the West ignores the commands of Allah revealed in the Koran. Others saw it as an attack on **American support of corrupt governments** in the Arab world, who they believe are supported and kept in power by America and Britain because of Western oil interests. Still others saw

Photo: REX FEATURES

September 11th 2001. Terrorist attack on the World Trade Centre

the attack on the World Trade Center as a fitting attack on the way America supports its own industries but demands "free trade" from those it buys goods from (see Chapter 12 on Institutional Evil for a further discussion of this). The people involved were heroes who would have preferred not to have hurt innocent victims but, given the innocent suffering caused in the world by American injustices, terrorism was justified. They would admit that those involved had lied to get on the planes that were hijacked but would say that sometimes it is right to lie in a good cause and that the group of people involved in the terrorist attacks showed great loyalty and support for each other as well as great courage.

Such a response, when faced with the charred remains of Americans being pulled from the rubble of the Trade Center, provoked a furious response. Indeed, some inside America who have tried to suggest that there is another side to the "evil terrorist" version of events have been issued with death threats.

The different perspectives are very hard indeed to reconcile but what is clear from this is that in the real world identifying evil is a far more complicated and hazardous matter than it would appear from the world of literature and film.

IS "EVIL" RELATIVE?

The above examples demonstrate how very difficult it is to talk in simplistic terms about where evil lies in complex modern day situations in the world. A very real alternative to trying to work out where the evil lies is to say that there is no such thing as evil. **Good and bad, right and wrong are all relative.** In other words in the above examples both sides are as bad as each other. It is six of one and half a dozen of the other! What a

• This Rwandan woman was one of more than 40 000 young Tutsi girls attacked and raped by the Hutu majority population of Rwanda.

• The Hutu majority called the Tutsis "cockroaches" and killed 800 000 of them within a month.

• The young boy was born as a result of the rape and the woman was too ashamed to face the camera when the picture was taken.

• Most people would consider that rape and genocide (seeking to destroy a whole race of people simply because they belong to that race) are evil and that this is not just a matter of personal opinion.

person regards as "evil" will depend on their situation and will be relative to their own experiences. This is a common perspective and means that most people do not have to engage with the problems. Applied to the above situations both America and the terrorists who bombed the Twin Towers are in the wrong. But neither will recognize this in themselves, they both blame the other. The Israelis and Palestinians are both in the wrong, but neither will recognize this about themselves. There is no difference between them. They are as bad as each other and in fact nobody is really evil. "Evil" does not exist as something we can identify and define; it just depends which side you are on, and is a word people use to blame others. The difference of perspective about what is and what is not evil has led some to argue that **"good" and "evil", "right" and "wrong" really just rests on a matter of opinion.**

This means that terrorists who bomb innocent Americans are not really doing anything wrong – the things they do are not liked by Americans, but that it just their perspective. Decisions by America to act or not act to support justice are neither right nor wrong, it is just the perspective that makes it so. Palestinians who choose to strap explosives to themselves and to self explode in Jewish areas are neither right nor wrong, good nor evil, it is just a matter of perspective. If you are a Palestinian it is a good thing to do, if you are a Jew it is a wicked thing to do.

Some hold that good and evil are purely a matter of our emotional reaction or the product of our upbringing. Some acts are merely called wrong because they are not liked within a particular society while other societies may find the same acts perfectly acceptable. Thus to be a suicide bomber is perfectly acceptable, indeed honourable, for a Palestinian, but Jewish people do not find it to their taste. To lead Jewish people to their deaths and then to use their hair to stuff mattresses is perfectly acceptable to one group of people but is not the preference of others. This argument holds that there is no real distinction between good and evil, and it is just a matter of what is accepted in society. When societies disagree and fighting or war breaks out there is no particular reason to look seriously at which side has justice or truth or goodness on its side, as there are no such things as justice, truth and goodness, any more than there are such things as evil, injustice and wickedness. It is all a matter of taste, preference and upbringing. (For a fuller discussion of this see Chapter Twelve.)

How easy is it to maintain this position in the following examples?

- *A professional drug trafficker organizes supplies of cocaine and heroin to be sold to the young people in your local town. They make a very great deal of money from doing this and do not appear to care that the lives of many people will be destroyed.*

- *A paedophile drives around your town in his Rolls Royce picking up young boys, taking them back to his flat and abusing them.*

- *A man beats and rapes his wife – hits her until she is disfigured, locks her in their house and treats her as a slave who has no freedom to leave the house.*

- *A political leader deliberately arranges a war with a neighboring country, in order to increase his popularity. Many thousands will die as a result.*

- *Two young boys, aged 10 and 9, take a little boy aged 3 away from his mother in a shopping mall. They go to a railway line, taunt him and then throw bricks and stones at him until first he stops screaming and then stops breathing.*

- *You notice that homosexuals, those with disabilities, communists and Jews are disappearing from your neighborhood. You do nothing to find out where they are taken, and do nothing to stop it continuing.*

- *You work for a multinational company. You need to cut the cost of producing training shoes in order to make more profit. If you cannot do this you will lose your job. You arrange for the shoes to be made in a poor country, where children will do most of the work. The factory will produce cheaply but has no health and safety measures for the children who work there and has no environmental protection. You know that some children will come to harm and that the environment will be damaged by the pollution caused by the factory.*

Most people would want to say that in these cases there is something going on that the word "evil" accurately describes. Most would want to say that there is a difference between good and evil, right and wrong, even if at times it is difficult to work it out. Most of us have never considered becoming involved in terrorist activities or any of the activities in the above list. We have not done anything like this, believe we would not do such things and do not consider ourselves evil. It is reassuring that these things are done by other people. But what about the following list?

- *Lying to save yourself from being in trouble.*
- *Cheating in a game.*
- *Taking something that does not belong to you because it was left lying around: "finders keepers".*
- *Gossiping about people who thought you were their friend.*
- *Pretending to like someone because they can be useful to you in some way.*
- *Noticing that someone needs help but not offering any.*
- *Wanting to hit someone or feeling like shouting at them.*
- *Wanting more money to buy things that are not really needed.*

Most would admit to recognizing themselves somewhere in the above list. It is less comfortable to recognize that "evil" may be a part of who we are and not just something done by other people, and so most people would not want to say that this is a list of "evil" things. However, the difference between the two lists may only be a matter of degree.

Talk of evil, however, assumes that there is a real distinction between good and evil and this is not just a matter of opinion. Most people would accept that there is a difference between good and evil, right and wrong, but this is not the same as saying what evil is and still less does it explain the source of evil. This book will explore the alternatives.

QUESTIONS FOR CONSIDERATION

1. How would you define evil?

2. Name two actions and two people whom you would describe as evil and explain why.

3. Can you think of anyone who would say that the acts listed on p17-18 were NOT evil? What reasons would they give?

4. Have you or anyone you know done anything that you would describe as evil? If so, what sort of thing was it?

5. How are EITHER Harry Potter and Malfoy OR Gandalf and Sauron different from each other?

CHAPTER TWO

WHERE DOES EVIL COME FROM?

The source of good and evil has been debated for thousands of years. Long before the Greek philosophers such as Socrates, Plato and Aristotle began the formal study of philosophy, the mystery of where evil came from was explored through story and myth. One of the most interesting and recurring ideas is that evil has its own independent power source; "evil" is a substance or a force and "good" also exists as a separate substance or force. All evil comes from this independent power and that is why there is evil in the world.

COSMIC DUALISM

A COSMIC dualist considers that there are two separate substances or two separate forces in the universe.

In the universe there are two cosmic principles of light and darkness. These two principles represent the two forces of good and evil and they eternally confront each other. They are engaged in cosmic warfare. Evil is at work in the world, but the principle of good is also equally at work. Neither side is stronger than the other and so good does not finally triumph over evil and evil does not triumph over good. It is a battle of two equal but opposite forces. Imagine two kittens in a house. They are equal in strength and mischievousness. The havoc they cause is immense, but they never seem to hurt each other! In cosmic dualism the two principles engage in cosmic warfare but neither side wins or loses. The universe, and our planet, is the battleground for these forces and their war creates terrible suffering and evil, but they themselves are hardly affected at all.

HUMAN DUALISM

Alongside this kind of dualism is human dualism. This belief is that human beings are also made of two principles or substances: body and soul. This is a very ancient belief.

Jaques-Louise David. The Death of Socates (1787)

This painting depicts the death of Socrates (469-399 BCE), a Greek Philosopher. He had been put on trial for perverting the youth of Athens – by making them think philosophically and therefore helping them to question and challenge the ideas of their parents – and had been condemned to death. He chose to die by drinking the poison hemlock, which is being handed to him in this picture by his friend. His friends asked what they should do with him when he had died and he laughed, "Do you think you will be able to catch me?" For Socrates the real "self" was his soul and on death this would separate and leave his body – the body that remained would rot and would be of no concern to him at all, as his real self had left to go before the judges who would judge his life. It was Plato (428-347 BCE), a student of Socrates, who wrote this account down and he was also a dualist maintaining that human beings have souls and bodies but the real "me" is my soul and it is the soul that survives death.

These two basic ideas, that there is an independent force of evil and that humans are made up of two substances, have been put together in a variety of ways by different dualists.

ZOROASTRIAN DUALISM

Zoroastrianism is perhaps the earliest religion that had dualism at its center. It was founded by **Zarathustra** and it is not certain when he lived. Estimates vary from about 6000 BCE to 600 BCE. On the basis of his style of writing and the language in which he wrote, the most popular date is sometime between 1500 and 1000 BCE. This means that Zoroastrian thinking was well formulated by the time that Buddhism, Christianity or Islam emerged and may well have influenced these major world religions. It also means that when the Jews were under Persian rule they too may have come into contact with Zoroastrian influences.

Zarathustra lived in Persia, modern day Iran. Stories say that his birth was predicted and that attempts were made by the forces of evil to kill him as a child. He preached belief in a single god when this idea was unheard of – every tribe had their own gods and his teaching was, therefore, very unpopular. However it finally gained the support of the king and Zoroastrianism become the official religion of the Persian Empire until Muslims invaded Persia in about 650 CE. A few Zoroastrians fled to India and today there are about 18000 of their descendents in India. Numbers are so small because being a Zoroastrian depends on descent – they do not make converts. Zoroastrianism may have been the first religion to believe in one God – although Christians, Jews and Muslims might hold that the story of Abraham pre-dates Zarathustra. Islam would fiercely reject the claim that Zarathustra was the first monotheist, as it is revealed in the sacred text of the Koran that Abraham was the first monotheist, that is the first person to reject all other gods and to hold there was one God alone. That Zoroastrians believe in one God does not mean that they are not dualists!

There are various schools of Zoroastrian thought but the main one holds that Ahura Mazda (Wise Lord) is an all-powerful God who is the only God worthy of worship. However Ahura Mazda created Ahirman who is a spirit of death and violence who fights against the good. Every person has to choose whether to follow the path of reality or unreality, as the universe is a battleground in which their struggle is worked out. Zoroastrians who support this view claim that eventually the good god will win and all evil will be destroyed leaving only goodness. This basic idea, however, gave rise to a whole series of more popular understandings. One understanding sees the supreme God, Ahura Mazda, as having two sons: Angra Mainya and Ahiram. The first chose "Good", the other chose "Evil", the destructive principle of greed, anger, and darkness. There is a constant fight between the two sons but at the end Good will triumph, there will be a "Final Judgment", the dead will be resurrected, and there will be a Paradise on earth. In some traditions there is a belief that a savior will be born, who will be a descendent of Zarathutsra, who will be born of a virgin. This man will raise the dead and conduct a final judgment.

The four most important legacies from Zoroastrianism are the ideas:

- *Of a dualistic struggle between good and evil. These are independent forces in the world*

- *Of a single God*

- *Of the resurrection of the dead*

- *Of judgment after death in which each has to account for their life*

It is possible that some of these ideas influenced Hebrew thinking particularly the later development of Jewish ideas of life after death. The Jewish people were under Persian rule between 536 BCE and 331 BCE. It seems likely that they would have come into close contact with Persian thinking during this period.

Zoroastrian dualism has it that there are two forces of good and evil. Humans can choose between these forces. Zoroastrian dualism also accepts human dualism; on death the soul separates from the body but at the time of judgment the person will experience bodily resurrection and judgment. The decisions made in this life will affect the judgment.

PLATO AND DUALISM

Plato considered that the world was created by the god whom Plato called the Demiurge. The Demiurge did not create the world out of nothing but fashioned raw, pre-existent matter, which was already in the universe. He did not create the original matter from which the universe was formed. The Demiurge used this pre-existent matter to shape the world and all things in it. The pattern for creation was found in the perfect Forms. These Forms exist as perfect ideas and all things are made in the image of a perfect Form. So, a horse is made in the image of the Form of a horse. The Form is absolutely perfect but the horse that is created is made from pre-existent matter and will change as it grows up and then gets old and dies. The created horse is not therefore perfect, unlike the Form of horse. For Plato there are Forms of all things. There is a Form of Truth, Justice, Goodness and Beauty. How does this work? Take the Form of Beauty, in this world we see examples of different beautiful things, for instance the beauty of a night sky, the beauty of a flower or of a baby's first cry. These are all called beautiful because, for Plato, they in some way resemble or participate in the perfect idea of Beauty that exists beyond time and space. The perfect Form of beauty exists and it is from the idea of the Form that we understand beauty and can say whether something is beautiful or not. Forms are written with a capital letter, so for example justice in the world resembles or participates in the "Form of Justice", which is real and exists as a perfect idea beyond time and space. These ideas were the models that the Demiurge used to make the universe.

This is where Plato's dualism emerges. Because the Demiurge had to use matter, which he did not create, the world he created was necessarily imperfect. The matter he used was chaotic matter and it resisted his will. All things that are made out of matter are therefore imperfect shadows of the Forms. Everything in space and time is changing and is a pale reflection of the perfection of the unchanging Forms. Evil, therefore, comes from the imperfection that flowed from the universe being in space and time and from it being created from pre-existent matter which resisted the Demiurge's will.

In Platonic thought there is a dualism between matter and non-matter. Matter is the source of all evil. In the case of a human being, the body is made of matter and the soul is not. The body is therefore created out of pre-existent chaotic matter and can persuade the soul, which inhabits the body, towards evil. Evil is built into the structure of the universe because it was made out of chaotic matter.

The combination of Platonic ideas and Zoroastrian dualism was to provide a potent mixture and influenced central ideas in the early centuries of Christianity.

Plato

CHRISTIAN NEO-PLATONIST DUALISM

Christian neo-Platonists were influenced by Plato's philosophy. The Forms, however, instead of existing as uncreated beyond time and space, were seen as perfect ideas in the mind of God. All notions of perfection such as horse, beauty, truth and justice exist in the mind of God. God is the source of all perfection, but is not directly responsible for creation and all of nature. The Forms represent the spiritual ideals of which all in creation is a shadow. Matter, including the human form, is imperfect and all that is of the flesh is imperfect. The challenge for Christian Neo-Platonists is to aspire to things of the spirit and to free themselves from things of the world. The movement towards the spiritual is a movement towards God and towards perfection, and is the path of goodness. Those who reject this choice remain in the shadows or in darkness as St John's gospel records. God is absolutely perfect and unchanging. Christian neo-Platonists absolve God from any responsibility for evil but at the price of making God very remote from the world, he did not even create it. **The dualism in neo-Platonism is between matter and spirit.** Matter is considered imperfect (at times they almost seemed to think that matter was evil) and the task is to purify the soul and not to let it be dragged down by sensual or other pleasures associated with matter. Only God is perfect and the attractions of the shadows of the world need to be resisted so that God alone is desired.

MANICHEAN DUALISM

The Manicheans were a group who challenged the early Christian church's understanding of the origin of evil with a theory of radical dualism, or division, not only between right and wrong, saints and sinners, light and darkness, but also between good and evil. Each of these, it was claimed, eternally confronts each other. Mani (215-277 CE) who founded the group was born into a Jewish Christian community in Persia. He preached a form of Christianity that placed an emphasis on reason and rejected a literal reading of the Bible. It incorporated many beliefs of Zoroastrianism and elements of Platonism. Mani taught that there were two basic principles in the cosmos - a principle of Light and a principle of Darkness. The principles of light and dark were in eternal combat. When an individual did something wrong they were not directly responsible but the principle of Darkness had taken them over. The Dark force was a far more powerful force than the individual human being and the cosmic combat was on going even in the lives of individuals. The good soul within each person was imprisoned in a "Realm of Darkness" that had invaded the "Realm of Light". Manichaeism promised that the good soul would eventually be set free and be reunited to its heavenly source. Mani taught that the way to the Realm of Light demanded the rejection of the pleasures of the flesh. Full members of his group had to become celibate and avoid all sensual and sexual activity. Those who followed his teachings were promised that they would become the elect (called "perfecti") so that after death they would ascend directly to the Kingdom of Light. Sensual and sexual activity were rejected as this was part of the material world and Mani taught that such things tied people down to a lesser reality than that achieved by the "perfecti". Everyone other than these elect would be reincarnated so that they would live through a whole series of lives until they advanced enough to become part of the elect.

The source of evil for Manichean dualists is due either to the work of the Evil Principle or to the work of this power within each human person. This was not accepted by those who believed in one all-powerful God as the Good Principle had no control or power over the Evil Principle. If there is only one all-powerful God then there has to be another explanation for the source of evil. There is further discussion on this in the following chapters.

GNOSTIC DUALISM

The Gnostics were another set of people who challenged Christian thinking about evil in the early years of the Christian church. The Gnostics believed in a very remote and unknowable High God (somewhat similar to the Zoroastrian Ahura Mazda). An angel of Wisdom, called Sophia, gave birth to the Demiurge (Lower God). This lower God, who the Gnostics considered was Jehovah in the Hebrew Scripture, was seen as an inferior God who was unaware of the existence of the High God and of his own mother Sophia. Jehovah created the earth, universe and human life, but his creation was defective and flawed. As a result, human life on earth is a form of Hell. Jesus came to earth to convey gnosis (specialized, **secret knowledge**) to a few select people. Jesus was not divine as he was made of matter, and matter for the Gnostic must be conquered before spiritual enlightenment can be gained. Knowledge could be given to individuals, but only very gradually and through a series of stages of achievement. Many of the requirements for those who wished to acquire further knowledge were concerned with the control of the flesh. Circumcision could be required and certain foods were forbidden.

The Gnostics maintained that only a select group had the gnosis or "inner knowledge" necessary for salvation – they formed an elect and everyone else would perish as they were dominated by the evil, material world and did not have the secret knowledge which was necessary to save them.

The Gnostics were dualists who believed that matter was evil and the spiritual side of human beings needed to be developed by rejecting the physical aspect. Most were expected to reject sex and even marriage as these would

John baptising Jesus

result in more material beings coming into the world. Others, who achieved the enlightenment of full spiritual knowledge, considered that they had risen above the material world and that it was no longer important. This led them to consider that sexual pleasure was perfectly acceptable as it involved matter and this was of no concern. **Gnostic dualism was a dualism between the spiritual and the physical and between knowledge and ignorance.**

DUALISM TODAY

Philosophic ideas rarely die. Dualism has great appeal even today and we do not have to go far to find its influence. As we have seen in the STAR WARS series there is a single spiritual force running through the universe and this force has two sides, both of which can be tapped and used by those who know how to do so. Training in the use of the force is long and hard but those who "let the force flow through them" or those who "are strong in the force" have tremendous power not available to ordinary people. Here we can see a dualistic view of the universe, with one force but two sides to it of Good and Evil.

Throughout the Harry Potter books the forces of Good and Evil are presented as being in constant combat with each other, and likewise in the Lord of the Rings. Evil is an active force which can take over the individual so that they are no longer in control of themselves. The nine wraiths, the Nazgul or dark lords who seek the ring and ride on horse back will never die, but they have given themselves over to the evil force so wholly that they are no longer recognisably human. They have no faces. The similarity with the "Dementors" in Harry Potter is striking. These pieces of literature are suggesting that evil is a force and that it is possible for evil to take over a person so completely that the person is almost destroyed. The person is no longer in control of themselves and in some ways is no longer really a human person (drugs can have this sort of impact). Not only this, and more frightening still, is the suggestion that they no longer have the power to become fully human again.

- This woman is bulimic.
- She looks at herself in the mirror and sees a fat person.
- She weighs less than five stones.
- When she eats she eats at least three meals worth of food at one go.
- She then feels guilty.
- She goes to the bathroom and makes herself vomit by sticking her toothbrush down her throat.
- She will do this repeatedly, often until her throat bleeds.

This dualistic view of the world is in some ways very appealing. What it means is that when a person does wrong things, or even things that we might call evil, it is not necessarily the fault of the individual. It is due to the presence within them of an evil power beyond their control. They cannot help but do the wicked things they do because the evil power is much stronger than they are. The Dualistic groups and the films that we have looked at have one more thing in common; each suggests that there is an equal but opposite power to the evil force, which is the power of good. This power is also at work in the world, and individuals can choose to work with the forces of good. In literature and films the two forces are not usually equal – good usually triumphs over evil BUT in a dualistic view of the world evil must triumph over good as many times as good triumphs over evil. This must be the case in a dualistic world where good and evil are equal forces in eternal conflict, otherwise good would eventually triumph. Even in very dark films, such as *The Silence of the Lambs* and *Pulp Fiction* there is a minor triumph of "good" in the end.

Dualism challenges us to ask whether there are forces at work in the world of Good and Evil. If there are, is it possible to resist the power of evil and choose the good? Or does evil take over a person? Dualism has never been accepted by Judaism, Christianity or Islam and in later chapters we will further explore why this is.

QUESTIONS FOR CONSIDERATION

1. Do you believe that there is an evil force in the world?

2. Can a person be so taken over by an "evil force" that they destroy themselves?

3. Are you convinced by "illnesses" such as cleptomania, where a person compulsively steals? Is it possible that the person has been taken over by an "evil force"?

4. Are you a dualist about human beings (in other words do you consider that human beings are made up of a soul and body and the soul separates on death)? Do you think that there is something "evil" about the body and the physical world?

5. Is it true, do you think, that sexual relationships make the development of a spiritual life more difficult?

6. Why have Christians always opposed cosmic dualism?

CHAPTER THREE

EVIL IN EASTERN TRADITIONS

Dualism provides one possible explanation for the source of evil in the world, but the Eastern traditions of Hinduism and Buddhism provide a possibly older and very different perspective. The Hindu and Buddhist approaches, instead of offering an explanation that involves a dualism between the forces of good and evil, offer a **choice between ignorance and knowledge.**

HINDUISM

Hinduism is a very ancient religion and has no identifiable founder – its origins lie in the mists of history. According to the Upanishads, some of the oldest Hindu scriptures written about 700 BCE, all things die and are reborn in an endless cycle. Behind all this change, however, is something which is not born and does not die and which remains timeless and unchanging – a supreme reality or Absolute. The goal of all existence is to escape from this changing world and to merge with the Absolute. This Absolute is represented by the three great figures of Brahma, Vishnu and Shiva – respectively Creator, Preserver and Destroyer (represented differently in the two pictures). These three together represent the one Absolute. The three form a unity, and this unity includes destruction and death.

The Law of Karma is a significant Hindu belief. It holds that every good or evil action has an inevitable effect. A person who does an evil action must suffer for it and a person who does a good action must get happiness as a result. This is an unbreakable law and nothing whatsoever can stop it happening. Every thought and every word contribute to an individual's "karma". Nothing

happens in the universe by chance or accident – there is a def-
inite connectedness between actions done now and a person's
future life. Bad actions and bad thoughts attract bad karma. It
is rather like a billiard ball view of the universe in which every
action is inevitably connected to an earlier one. Nothing can
cancel out bad "Karma", but it is possible to attract good karma
as well with positive thoughts and good actions.

Brahma, Vishnu and Shiva

Hinduism recognizes that virtuous people often suffer in this
life and evil people often succeed and prosper. The belief in
reincarnation, or re-birth of a person into a new body after
death, explains this – **Karma affects future lives** and not just this life. If a
person dies with a debt of bad karma they may be reborn lower down the
human scale or if they were at the bottom of the scale already they can be reborn as an animal. Human beings are at the highest point on the Hindu scale
of life, but some humans are regarded as better than others by birth. There
are grades of human beings and in the next life a person can go up or down
the human scale; this is called a caste system. Brahmins are born into the
highest caste and this is because of the effects of their good deeds in previous lives. The "untouchables", by contrast, are the lowest caste and are born
in this state either because they have been wicked in past lives and have
therefore regressed in the chain of being or else because they were previous-
ly animals. The "untouchables" are at the bottom of the caste system and also
at the bottom of the social scale – they do tasks such as cleaning toilets or
handling dead bodies which others would not do and this is justified because
of their past lives.

There are some 3000 castes and it is today debated whether the caste system
is essential to Hinduism – critics claim that it is a religious means of keeping
the rich and wealthy (the Brahmins) in positions of power and wealth whilst
at the same time offering comfort to those at the bottom of the heap with
promises of a reward in future lives if they do not accumulate bad karma and
have desires above their station in life.

Hinduism holds that everyone dies with unfulfilled desires and these desires
contribute to karma. If the desires are selfish and evil then the person will be
born at a lower point in the great chain of being, but if the desires are good,
then the person will progress. What is more, karma affects a person's desires
for good or evil. Sometimes a person can be born with both good and evil

desires and this represents the effects of karma from a life lived with a mixture of good and evil deeds, thoughts and desires in previous lives.

Every action a person does, according to Hinduism, has three effects:

1. *The action produces an appropriate reward or punishment either in this life or after death.*

2. *The action leaves behind an impression in a person's mind, which will make it easier for the person to repeat the action (for good or ill) in the future. The impressions left in the mind are called chitta and these are stored as subtle impressions – samskaras.*

3. *These impressions, both good as well as bad, bind the person to this world and they are compelled to be reborn again and again until all samskaras or karmas are exhausted or worked out.*

Evil is real but it depends very much on the perspective from which it is seen and, at the highest level, evil does not exist. A great modern Hindu guru, Sri Ramakrishna, said:

"Evil exists in God as poison in a serpent. What is poison to us is not poison to the serpent. Evil is evil only from the point of view of man."

This does not deny that people experience the reality of evil, but says that from the point of view of the Absolute, it does not exist. When a wicked thing is done it is done out of selfishness. Selfish actions are evil actions, such as:

• *Those actions rooted in sensual pleasure*

• *Actions that only benefit small numbers of people or one's family or*

• *All actions of deceit or corruption*

BUT WHAT MAKES THEM EVIL IS THE EFFECT THEY HAVE ON THE PERSON PERFORMING THE ACTION. Selfish, evil behaviour takes a person away from knowledge of the Absolute and into a state of ignorance. Evil is living in this state of ignorance. Evil is due to the law of karma which means that it is not random. Even this, whilst viewed as evil by the one who suffers it, is not viewed as evil from the perspective of the Absolute. Good and Evil are not active powers in the world but are words used to describe actions that bring each person closer to self-realization. Evil actions are selfish actions. **There is no concept of sinfulness as in Christianity since every person is struggling to be free. People are not sinful but ignorant and what is required is to proceed from ignorance to a true understanding.**

All religions can be misinterpreted from outside by those who do not understand the myths and symbols which make up the religion. It is easy for the non-Christian to misunderstand Christian symbols and the same certainly applies in the case of Hindu images. The images of the Hindu gods are, to Western eyes, grotesque and perhaps primitive but this attitude represents a failure of understanding of the symbolism – as in the case of the paintings and statues of Kali and Shiva (see box).

The scriptures of the great Hindu Brahmins contains profound moral sayings concerning selflessness and restraint, yet the most popular gods, such as Vishnu and Shiva are not identified with any moral law or principle. They stand above morality where there is no good or evil. Morality is, however, a fundamental law of the universe as it is based on karma – evil actions cause the person to move further away from personal fulfill-

Kali and Shiva

Kali is shown standing on the prostrate form of her husband, Shiva. Kali has four arms and these:

1. Hold the sword of death – this represents spiritual discipline and the need for her followers to die to the sensual pleasures of the world,

2. Hold the blood dripping human head – this tells the worshipper that only by losing one's life will one find it.

3. Makes the gesture of "Fear Not" – shows that the goddess protects her children and what appears to be evil on earth is actually a part of the overall cosmic unity of good and evil.

4. Makes the gesture of "Bestowing gifts" to indicate the protection that worshippers will receive.

The image of Kali standing on Shiva who is lying on the ground appears to show that Kali has vanquished Shiva. This is far too simple, however, because Kali can also be seen as the dream of Shiva who is asleep. Shiva and Kali together represent two sides of the one reality.

One reason why some Hindu statues often represent the sexual act is that this is seen as bringing together the masculine and the feminine, uniting the contraries as good and evil are united in the cosmos. The distinction between male and female disappears in the Hindu idea of the Absolute.

ment. In the end, therefore, what is right or wrong depends on what furthers the development of human beings.

Traditional Hinduism sees the world in negative terms and thinks it is better to leave the world to move towards union with the Absolute or God. There is little attempt to explain why the world should be the way it is – it is rather like a scientist exploring the laws of nature without considering why they exist. Similarly Hinduism is, effectively, the science of karma. Most Hindu thinkers do not, therefore, consider the reasons for evil. The seventh-century Tamil poet Appar summarized this negative view of human existence:

"Evil, all evil, my race, evil my qualities all, Great am I only in sin, evil is even my good.
Evil my innermost self, foolish, avoiding the pure.
Beast am I not, yet the ways of the beast I can never forsake
I can exhort with strong words, telling men what they should hate,
Yet I can never give gifts, only to beg them I know.
Ah! wretched man that I am, where unto came I to birth?"

Traditional Hinduism holds that only the elite, the Brahmins, could hope to achieve release from the endless round of rebirth and merge with the Absolute – and it would take many, many lifetimes to become a Brahmin. For everyone else, there was no escape. Modern day Hinduism is rather more positive about the world and a concentration on material success and doing well has in popular religion become substituted for the original idea of seeking release from the world.

In summary for the HINDU the source of evil is ignorance of the Absolute.

BUDDHISM

Siddhartha was born in the mid-sixth century BCE in Kapilavastu in northeast India close to Tibet. The title "Buddha" was given to him when he became enlightened. Prior to his enlightenment he was what subsequently came to be referred to as a BODHISATTVA. His father ruled a kingdom in Northern India and he lived in the royal palace.

When he was a child a holy man prophesied that he would either become a

great prince like his father or, if he saw certain sights including suffering and death, he
would become a holy man. His father therefore did everything to keep him in his castle
and he was surrounded by luxury. He married at 16 and had every material thing his
heart could desire. As the Buddha himself
said "I was spoilt, very spoilt". The story
goes that one day he left the castle and saw
the negativities of life – sickness, suffering
and death – and he then left the castle and
pursued the life of a wandering holy man
seeking wisdom. He eventually attained
enlightenment and, when later disciples
asked him "Are you a God?" he would say
"No, I am awake". The Buddha saw his task
as being to wake other people up.

*The Budda is not a god but a human
who achieved enlightenment, and is
'awake'*

Like Hinduism, Buddhism holds that we are bound by the iron law of KARMA.
We suffer, and others are caused to suffer, because of the three great roots of
evil. These are:

1. *Greed – wanting our own way, acting out of desire or selfishness*

2. *Ill-will – wanting ill for other people either as we wish to take revenge
   because we have been hurt or because we do not like a person or feel
   negatively towards them because of some factor such as race, colour,
   religious grouping, sexuality, possessions, behaviour or the like*

3. *Delusion – acting out of instinct because we are ignorant, because we do
   not understand the forces acting on us, or the reasons why we act as we do.*

When any actions are motivated by these forces, then there are bound to be
negative and evil consequences.

When the Buddha achieved enlightenment he came to understand the real
state of the world as a place that was full of suffering. His enlightenment
enabled him to see how this suffering could be avoided. He was tempted by a
figure called Mara - some Buddhists see this as a devil type figure but others

Seeking Understanding

In the case of the September 11 2001 attacks on the Twin Towers in New York, the Buddhist would look at the causes of resentment in the Arab world, for instance:

- At the anger caused by the creation of the State of Israel which resulted in tens of thousands going into refugee camps.

- At the lack of justice in allowing Israel to ignore United Nations resolutions which condemned their taking of territory which did not belong to them.

- At the continual financial and military support given to Israel by which the US allows it to attack with impunity any neighbouring state which supports the Palestinians.

- At the bombing by the West of those who disagree with them without considering dispassionately the justice of the dispute.

- At the selfishness of the West regarding oil

- At the arrogance of the West about the rightness of their own culture.

would see Mara as the personification of the evil side of human nature. Mara is the great confuser of humanity and it is the teaching of the Buddha and his followers that Mara can be overcome.

The Buddhist view of evil is not to see it in any way as a force opposed to good. There is no God in Buddhism and no mysterious forces. Instead **evil is located within human beings and the results of their actions** when they act in certain ways. The most serious problem is ignorance because human beings do not know or do not understand the forces that make them act as they do. Secondly evil is caused by desire; desire is something that each individual must rid themselves of. The first step, therefore, to combating evil for the Buddhist is for each individual to **move away from ignorance to self-understanding.** Understanding why a person acts as they do is the first step to overcoming the evil they do. (There are obvious links here with the Western emphasis on the importance of psychology in helping to understand the motives for actions.)

The Buddhist Peace Fellowship reacted to the events of September 11 when the US Twin Towers were destroyed by saying:

"Nations deny causality by ascribing blame to others' terrorists, rogue nations, and so on. Singling out an enemy, we short-circuit the introspection necessary to see our own karmic responsibility for the terrible acts that have befallen us ... Until we own causes we bear responsibility for, in this case in the Middle East, last week's violence will make no more sense than an earthquake or cyclone, except that in its human origin it turns us toward rage and revenge."

The Buddhist response to the September 11 attack is to understand the motives and to acknowledge that there is responsibility on both sides. It was not an action that came from an evil force outside of human nature; it was simply the consequence of human action. Humans are the source of evil. Evil comes because of desires and a failure to understand what motivates ourselves and others.

For the Buddhist, the first step in responding to evil done by others should be to try to understand why they acted as they did. Instead of immediately demonizing them, the Buddhist would seek to understand their motivations. Once this understanding is reached it becomes possible to see why those who attacked the Twin Towers of New York acted as they did. The Buddhist would see the seeds of evil lying in human actions and if any country, society or individual acts out of greed, ill will or from delusion then evil consequences will result.

For the Buddhist the way to overcome evil is to:

1. *Understand what gave rise to the evil in the first place, and then*

2. *To absorb the evil and to refuse to let it continue its cycle of damage. This means refusing to retaliate, forgiving people who do wrong, thinking the best of people who hurt you (and this becomes easier once one understands why they act as they do).*

Individual Buddhists will do the same with their own actions – starting not by condemning themselves but by trying to understand why they have acted as they have done. This can be hard and it is often painful. St Paul put it well when he said "The good that I would, I do not and the evil that I would not, that I do". The Buddhist would agree with this but would say the crucial matter is to understand why we acted wrongly. Only then can change become possible. If we just condemn ourselves and "beat ourselves up" when we do wrong, then no change will take place. It is only when we take time to understand ourselves that change becomes possible.

Delusion has a special meaning in Buddhism. The most important delusion comes when individuals do not understand that they are a part of the world in which they live and their actions have consequences on others as well as on themselves. Once they feel that they are separated from others so that an

Try sitting on the floor in a place that is quiet and peaceful. If you are inside, light a candle and place it on the floor just in front of you. If you are outside, pick up a leaf or a stone and hold it in your hands. Now try concentrating and thinking ONLY of the candle or the leaf or the stone for five minutes.

Most of us will be unable to do this, as our mind will "wander off". This is what Buddhists mean when they say that our minds are not under our control.

We are not our minds. We can control our minds and only when we do so can we control our actions and then try to stop acting selfishly and thus causing hurt and damage to people.

"us and them" mentality emerges, then this causes suffering.

For Buddhism, the way to overcome suffering is to first of all gain knowledge of ourselves. If we cannot understand ourselves or why we act then we certainly will not be able to understand others or why they act. It is here that meditation comes in. Buddhists will spend long periods in silent meditation, being still and focusing on a candle or concentrating on their breathing. Being still and meditating is a vital and essential part of coming to understand the self and of taking control of the self. For the Buddhist if a person cannot even control the mind then they certainly cannot control their actions and this leads, in Buddhist thought, to people acting out of pure instinct, without thought or reflection. It is not surprising when they do this that "evil" consequences arise.

"Our mind is out of control. It is just like a monkey jumping about senselessly. It goes upstairs, gets bored, runs back downstairs, gets tired of that, goes to the movie, gets bored again, has good food or poor food, gets bored with that." (Ajahn Chah, "A Still Forest Pool")

The aim of meditation is to control the mind, not to let it control you. For the Buddhist we are more than just the mind – the mind can be controlled and directed. The aim is to find peace and stillness – and through this wisdom or enlightenment.

Meditation is the way the individual frees

him or herself from distractions, finds an inner vision and enlightenment about the true nature of the world. As such, meditation has no ethical value in itself – it is a means to knowledge and control of the self, and freedom from desires – this is how the individual is released from evil thoughts and actions. Through meditation human beings can first recognize how they are influenced by emotions such as anger, greed and hatred and then, having recognized these, can seek to overcome them. Evil results when these emotions are given free reign. A Buddhist will, therefore, not react out of instinct, anger or desire but will only act after a period of reflection in which they first understood their reactions and why they feel as they do. They will then try to understand the actions and feelings of others. The aim will be to absorb and accept evil and not to allow any thought or action they do to perpetuate it.

Buddhists, therefore, locate evil firmly in the human psyche and believe that it is caused by ignorance of the self. It is this that needs to be overcome. There is no God, no transcendent order of value but the effects of evil are nevertheless real and need to be overcome.

QUESTIONS FOR CONSIDERATION

1. Hinduism does not seek to explain where evil comes from. Is there any need to do this?

2. In what way is the Hindu understanding of evil linked to the Indian caste system?

3. Buddhism does not have any idea of a God who creates and sustains the universe. What effects does this have on the Buddhist understanding of the source of evil?

4. Imagine you are a Buddhist. You are in a war situation and soldiers are attacking your brother or sister. You have a gun. What is your approach as a Buddhist?

5. What might Buddhist attitudes be to living in a society where the poor do not have enough to eat and starvation and child labour are common?

THE SOURCE OF EVIL IN THE CHRISTIAN TRADITION

From Genesis to St Thomas Aquinas via St Augustine

There are two creation stories in the Book of Genesis and modern scholars consider that they were written about four hundred years apart, (the earlier account in Genesis 2-3 in 950 BCE and the later account found in Genesis 1 in 550 BCE.) These stories have had a massive impact on the understanding about evil the West. It is easy to dismiss myth and story as "just a myth" or "just a story" but this is a failure to appreciate the very deep truths that a story can communicate and the power a story can have to capture spiritual truth. The reason these two accounts have had such an impact upon Western understanding about evil is not because all Christians believe every word of the Bible, and therefore think that they are literally true. A story does not have to be literally true to contain truth. It is the recognition that these accounts accurately reflect deep spiritual truth that gives them their enduring appeal and power, even today.

The second Creation story (Gen.2:4b – 25)

This is the account of the heavens and the earth when they were created.
When the LORD God made the earth and the heavens and no shrub of the field
had yet appeared on the earth and no plant of the field had yet sprung up, for
the LORD God had not sent rain on the earth and there was no man to work
the ground, but streams came up from the earth and watered the whole surface
of the ground the LORD God formed the man from the dust of the ground and
breathed into his nostrils the breath of life, and the man became a living
being. Now the LORD God had planted a garden in the east, in Eden; and there
he put the man he had formed. And the LORD God made all kinds of trees grow
out of the ground – trees that were pleasing to the eye and good for food. In
the middle of the garden were the tree of life and the tree of the knowledge of
good and evil. A river watering the garden flowed from Eden; from there it was
separated into four headwaters. The name of the first is the Pishon; it winds
through the entire land of Havilah, where there is gold. (The gold of that land
is good; aromatic resin and onyx are also there.) The name of the second river
is the Gihon; it winds through the entire land of Cush. The name of the third
river is the Tigris; it runs along the east side of Asshur. And the fourth river is
the Euphrates. The LORD God took the man and put him in the Garden of Eden
to work it and take care of it. And the LORD God commanded the man, "You
are free to eat from any tree in the garden; but you must not eat from the tree
of the knowledge of good and evil, for when you eat of it you will surely die."
The LORD God said, "It is not good for the man to be alone. I will make a
helper suitable for him." Now the LORD God had formed out of the ground all
the beasts of the field and all the birds of the air. He brought them to the man
to see what he would name them; and whatever the man called each living
creature, that was its name. So the man gave names to all the livestock, the
birds of the air and all the beasts of the field. But for Adam no suitable helper
was found. So the LORD God caused the man to fall into a deep sleep; and
while he was sleeping, he took one of the
man's ribs and closed up the place with
flesh. Then the LORD God made a woman
from the rib he had taken out of the man,
and he brought her to the man. The man
said, "This is now bone of my bones and
flesh of my flesh; she shall be called
'woman', for she was taken out of man." For
this reason a man will leave his father and
mother and be united to his wife, and they
will become one flesh. The man and his wife
were both naked, and they felt no shame.

This second account, the earlier of the two, records the perfect creation of the world, again, but adds to it an account of the lives of the first people, Adam and Eve. The key elements are as follows:

- *It pictures God creating a world out of nothing. There was no life at all before God's direct act of creation. God is the source of all things and there is no evil*

- *Man, Adam, was formed from the earth and life was breathed into him directly by God. The Hebrew word for "breathed into" can be translated as "spirited into". This story is claiming that in a real sense, humans, although made from the dust of the earth, have the spirit of God in them.*

- *Man was created first and afterwards plants and then animals. Adam names the animals in an act of stewardship and dominion.*

- *The man, by himself, is placed in a garden – Eden, meaning Paradise – and is given the command not to eat from the tree of knowledge. This was the only command God gave. Such a simple command to keep and yet it would be so easy to disobey. Woman is created when Adam is lonely and in need of companionship which the animals cannot provide. She is made out of Adam's rib. It is a mistake to read this as "man came first and woman as an afterthought". In the original Hebrew, "adam" is a word for which there is no direct English equivalent. The nearest might be "earth creature". "Adam" is not sexual – it is only after the "adam" is put to sleep that "is" (the Hebrew for man) and "issa" (the Hebrew for women) are created. Adam is best understood in the same way the word "mankind" is used – as inclusive of male and female principles.*

- *Adam names "Eve" – the act of naming her is the only indication in this text of any supremacy of the male over the female.*

The first story of creation was, modern scholars consider, written LATER than the second. It was probably written during the Babylonian captivity after Jerusalem had fallen about 596-587 BCE and when the people of Israel were taken into captivity by the Babylonians. It again tells the story of creation but there are significant differences from the earlier story. In this account it is God's creative WORD that causes creation - God brings the world into existence by his direct command. God's WORD was seen as coming to the Hebrew

The first Creation story (Gen: 1.1 - 2 4a)

In the beginning God created the heavens and the earth. Now the earth was formless and empty, darkness was over the surface of the deep, and the Spirit of God was hovering over the waters. And God said, "Let there be light," and there was light. God saw that the light was good, and he separated the light from the darkness. God called the light "day", and the darkness he called "night". And there was evening, and there was morning – the first day. And God said, "Let there be an expanse between the waters to separate water from water." So God made the expanse and separated the water under the expanse from the water above it. And it was so. God called the expanse "sky". And there was evening, and there was morning – the second day. And God said, "Let the water under the sky be gathered to one place, and let dry ground appear". And it was so. God called the dry ground "land", and the gathered waters he called "seas". And God saw that it was good. Then God said, "Let the land produce vegetation: seed-bearing plants and trees on the land that bear fruit with seed in it, according to their various kinds." And it was so. The land produced vegetation: plants bearing seed according to their kinds and trees bearing fruit with seed in it according to their kinds. And God saw that it was good. And there was evening, and there was morning – the third day. And God said, "Let there be lights in the expanse of the sky to separate the day from the night, and let them serve as signs to mark seasons and days and years, and let there be lights in the expanse of the sky to give light on the earth." And it was so. God made two great lights – the greater light to govern the day and the lesser light to govern the night. He also made the stars. God set them in the expanse of the sky to give light on the earth, to govern the day and the night, and to separate light from darkness. And God saw that it was good. And there was evening, and there was morning – the fourth day. And God said, "Let the water teem with living creatures, and let birds fly above the earth across the expanse of the sky." So God created the great creatures of the sea and every living and moving thing with which the water teems, according to their kinds, and every winged bird according to its kind. And God saw that it was good. God blessed them and said, "Be fruitful and increase in number and fill the water in the seas, and let the birds increase on the earth." And there was evening, and there was morning – the fifth day. And God said, "Let the land produce living creatures according to their kinds: livestock, creatures that move along the ground, and wild animals, each according to its kind." And it was so. God made the wild animals according to their kinds, the livestock according to their kinds, and all the creatures that move along the ground according to their kinds. And God saw that it was good. Then God said, "Let us make man in our image, in our likeness, and let them rule over the fish of the sea and the birds of the air, over the livestock, over all the earth, and over all

The first Creation story (continued)

the creatures that move along the ground." So God created man in his own image, in the image of God he created him; male and female he created them. God blessed them and said to them, "Be fruitful and increase in number; fill the earth and subdue it. Rule over the fish of the sea and the birds of the air and over every living creature that moves on the ground." Then God said, "I give you every seed-bearing plant on the face of the whole earth and every tree that has fruit with seed in it. They will be yours for food. And to all the beasts of the earth and all the birds of the air and all the creatures that move on the ground – everything that has the breath of life in it – I give every green plant for food." And it was so. God saw all that he had made, and it was very good. And there was evening, and there was morning – the sixth day. Thus the heavens and the earth were completed in all their vast array. By the seventh day God had finished the work he had been doing; so on the seventh day he rested from all his work. And God blessed the seventh day and made it holy, because on it he rested from all the work of creating that he had done.

Prophets and in John's Gospel it is God's WORD that becomes flesh in Jesus. The story is told of God creating the world in seven "days" – even for those who take the Bible literally, this does not necessarily mean "days" as we understand the term – after all the sun and moon are not created till the third day. This story differs significantly from the second, earlier, story:

- *God appears to be bringing order out of chaos. There is already formless matter before God starts to create. It is as if God is a sculptor moulding the universe out of matter (clay) that was already there.*

- *God divides land from water and it is God, who gives names to that which he creates.*

- *On the second day God creates the sun and the moon. This story was written during the exile of the people of Israel in Babylon. The Babylonians worshipped the sun and the moon as gods and one reason for this story having Israel's God create the sun and the moon is to emphasise that these are created things and are dependent on God. The point of the story would have been clear to readers at the time – even those things that the Babylonians worshipped as gods were made by Israel's God.*

- *Constantly the story repeats how good God considers the creation to be. God takes delight in God's creation – this culminates at the end of the story in God looking at everything that has been made and seeing it as "very good".*

- *God creates sea creatures and birds first and next land creatures. There is no idea here of evolution at work – this is a story told by devout believers trying to express truths about the creation of the world by. It was created by God and is dependant on God for all good things.*

- *Human beings are created in the image of God – this is different from the second story which had humans created from dust. Male and female are created together. Male and female TOGETHER are in the image of God. This is a way of saying that there is a part of human beings that is spiritual and properly belongs to God. Humans have something in them that means that they will not feel complete and at peace unless this spiritual longing is recognized. This is very simular to saying that God breathed a spirit into material things. It is the spirit of God that animates a human person in the second account which is also a way of saying that there is something essential in human beings that of God*

In both the second and first creation stories, humans and animals are portrayed as vegetarians – they eat only plants. The picture painted in each is of a state of paradise where there is no killing and "the wolf and the lamb lie down together". In both these stories, human beings are created in the presence of God – God takes delight in God's creation.

Michelangelo's picture of creation (in the Sistine Chapel in St Peter's in Rome) portrays this. Adam is physically beautiful – God's touch brings Adam to life and Adam can see God directly. Indeed Adam is effectively painted by Michelangelo as a younger version of God.

Adam is, of course, naked and unashamed – he is perfect and beautiful; totally what God intended. In this state of perfection Adam and God look at each other directly.

Michaelangelo. God creating Adam

THE INTRODUCTION OF EVIL

Having told the story of how human life was meant to be the writers of the Genesis stories account for the great disorders in the world – human shame, fear and separation from God. A number of aetiological myths are included in the narrative. (An aetiological myth is a narrative designed to explain an observed fact or phenomenon), but the main thrust of the story is directed at the question; **if God created the world, and all things in it good, where did evil and suffering come from?** If God were good he would not allow it; if God were all-powerful he would do something to stop it.

The Snake

In the garden is a snake. The snake is not evil or demonic, but part of God's creation. It is clever, and provides the stimulus for Eve to freely choose to eat. The serpent does not make her eat, but appeals to her reason:

"You will not die. For God knows that when you eat of it your eyes will be opened, and you will be like God, knowing good and evil." (Genesis 3:5)

The serpent represents reason; he tries to convince the woman that she can understand God better from the neutral stance of cold reason than from the position of trust and obedience. Eve in the story listens to the snake, eats the forbidden fruit and offers it to Adam. Evil is introduced into the world not by God, but by the free choice of Eve, and then by Adam. According to this myth all evil in the world stems from the use of reason over faith and trust in God. The use of reason to assert self-will over the will of God breaks down any relationship with God.

Knowledge of Good and Evil

The serpent tells Eve that she will not die if she eats the fruit, and in the story Adam and Eve do not immediately die. The direct consequences of the act are that they feel shame (v37) and fear God (v38). They are called to explain themselves and each tries to pass the blame back on to God as clever children try to blame a parent for their wrong doings. "The woman whom you gave to be with me. "explains Adam, "The serpent" (who you made), "beguiled me," explains Eve. The immediate punishment in fact turns out to be something worse than bodily death; from now on their minds will be in constant enmity with God, for they will know the difference between good and evil. To have knowledge of good and evil means to have experience of good and evil

Michaelangelo. Temptation and expulsion of Adam and Eve. On the right, Adam and Eve cowering before the angel with the sword

and the capacity to choose whether to follow the will of God or one's own mind. Knowledge of good and evil here means being given the capacity to take their lives into their own hands.

In the garden they were children, now they have to take responsibility for themselves, their decisions and their behaviour. This is seen in the Jewish tradition as a gift, but in the Christian tradition as "the fall".

The aetiological motifs in this story, which are posed as solutions to the questions about why things are the way they are include: why do we feel ashamed of our nakedness; why do we wear clothes; why is there such pain in childbirth; why does the earth not give food easily; why does the snake have no legs; why is knowing God such a struggle?

The Grace of God

"And the Lord God made for Adam and for his wife garments of skin, and clothed them" (Genesis 3:21)

The snake is cursed by God but Adam and Eve are not. They are accepted, in their shame and nakedness, and God acts to preserve them. God has not created only to walk away; He is intimately involved with his creation. Grace is a part of the nature of God; he is gracious in his forgiveness and faithful in his love. Making skins for Adam and Eve to wear is a symbol of this. Evil exists in the world but only in human free choices – it is not a power – the world is still the creation of God.

The source of evil is human beings – not God or an independent force of evil or pre-existent matter. Later Christian theology was to see the serpent as the devil, but this is not the way the Biblical writers themselves see it.

The fruit that is eaten is not an apple in the Hebrew. This seems to be a tradition that arose from the Latin translation: malus = bad, malum = apple.

Michelangelo portrays the devil as a woman (this was normal in art in the middle ages when women were seen as one of the chief means used by the devil to lead men astray - this was because they were considered to be so attractive that men would be tempted to sexual activity which was forbidden. Indeed St Augustine held that it was the devil who introduced sexual pleasure – in the garden of Eden there would have been no pleasure involved in sex. Michelangelo shows the serpent's coils merging into a woman's body.)

It could seem to an observer that God was being unreasonable – after all why shouldn't the woman have eaten the fruit? She wanted to gain wisdom, and what is wrong with that? We have in this story a theme that runs throughout the Hebrew Scriptures – namely that obedience to God is absolutely central. Self-will and the use of reason can be used to justify disobedience. This is probably the single most important message of the whole of the Hebrew Scriptures.

Because of the disobedience of Eve and Adam, evil enters the world and as a result the couple are driven out of the Garden of Eden and have to cope with a world which is now flawed.

The torments of hell

Pain and suffering, hard work and affliction

all enter the world for the first time. The message of the Biblical writers is clear – human beings have brought evil and suffering on themselves through the actions of Eve and Adam and the effects these actions have had on their descendants. Michelangelo (in the painting on p.47) portrays Adam and Eve being expelled from Eden. Eve cowers behind Adam as if feeling guilty because of their actions whilst Michelangelo's Adam is almost defiant and yet they are both resigned to their fate. An angel has a drawn sword indicating the permanent expulsion of the couple from paradise.

ST AUGUSTINE

St Augustine was one of the greatest figures in Christian history. He was Bishop of Hippo at a particularly difficult time and led quite an eventful life as a young man (he had a child by his long term mistress but never married and devoted his life wholly to the church once he had became a Bishop). Augustine used these stories to explain evil in theological terms. Augustine at times appears to take the Genesis stories literally, although as a scholar the literal reading of scripture troubled him. God, Augustine accepted, created the world perfect and never intended there to be earthquakes, floods, disease, cruelty or, indeed, for animals to eat each other. Adam and Eve caused evil to enter the world by their wilful disobedience.

St Augustine considered there were two types of evil – moral evil where human beings choose to act wrongly (represented by the painting "The torments of hell" where those who have sinned are sent to Hell) and natural evil where natural disasters and diseases cause suffering.

St Augustine formulated his approach to evil against a background of reacting against the semi-Christian group, the Manichaeans. They were DUALISTS and held that there were two opposed forces in the Universe - GOOD and EVIL. These two opposed forces were involved in a cosmic war with each other. The Evil force was responsible for all the evil in the world. They supported their claims with quotations from the Bible such as the Book of Revelation which has St Michael and his angels going out to do battle with the devil and his angels – almost like two opposed powers (The Star Wars films portray today the same idea of a cosmic struggle between good and evil).

St Augustine, however, recognized that this was not a Christian position. Christians, Muslims and Jews hold that there is one God who created the whole universe – **there is no independent power of evil because all that is was created by God.** What is more, this God is wholly good and all-powerful. How, then, could Augustine reply to the Manicheans in their claim that evil was to be explained in terms of an independent principle or power of evil? It seemed as though the only way forward was to accept that either God was not all good or God was not omnipotent. Augustine's genius was to avoid this dilemma. He did so by using the philosophy of Aristotle.

Aristotle was one of the greatest (possibly the greatest) of the Greek philosophers and his influence on later Christian thought has been enormous. Aristotle held that various negative things could be defined by the absence of some good to which they corresponded. For instance:

- *Darkness is an absence of light. Where there is no light, there is darkness.*

- *Poverty is an absence of wealth. Where there is little or no wealth there is poverty.*

- *Sickness is an absence of health. Where health is not present, there is sickness.*

He gives a famous example of a pilot whose job it is to guide a ship safe into a harbour. If the pilot does not join the ship, then the ship will be wrecked. The wreck was, therefore, caused by the absence of the pilot. The pilot did not do anything (for instance he was not drunk on duty and thus steered the ship badly), he simply was not there, and because of his absence the ship was wrecked. Evil occurs, therefore, where some good should be present (in this case the presence of the pilot on the bridge of the ship) and in fact it is absent.

St Augustine took this philosophical concept and applied it to the idea of evil. Goodness consisted in order and harmony – things were good if they fulfilled their nature. Evil, therefore, represented disorder and lack of harmony and, in particular, where some good that belonged to the nature of a thing was missing.

Augustine followed Aristotle and held that evil is not a positive thing in itself – rather EVIL IS AN ABSENCE OF GOOD. However it is not every absence that is an evil, and Augustine made a vital distinction between ABSENCE and PRIVATION.

- *An ABSENCE occurs where some good is absent which should not be there in the first place. For instance a stone cannot see. A stone, therefore, has an absence of eyes. A donkey cannot fly, the donkey has an absence of wings.*

- *A PRIVATION occurs where some good is absent which a thing SHOULD have. If a donkey cannot see, then this is a privation as a donkey should be able to see. If a seagull has no wings, this is a privation as a seagull should be able to fly.*

When something FALLS SHORT of what it should be, it suffers a privation. Thus a blind donkey or a wingless seagull would both be suffering a privation. For St Augustine, any privation is evil – to the extent that anything falls short of what it should be, it suffers a privation. There could be innumerable examples:

- *A dog that has lost its tail, suffers a privation. It is missing the tail that it should have and is therefore suffering an evil.*

- *An octopus without a tentacle suffers a privation. It is missing a tentacle that it should have and is therefore suffering an evil.*

- *A human being who is deaf suffers a privation. The person is missing the ability to hear which a human being should be able to do and is, therefore, suffering an evil.*

- *A human with Downs Syndrome suffers a privation, as he or she is less than perfectly what it is to be a human being.*

Lying behind this whole approach is the idea that every plant and animal (including humans) have a distinctive God-given nature and to the extent that anything falls short of what its nature should be it suffers a privation – it is not as it should be and to that extent is evil.

However, St Augustine considered that angels and human beings are different from everything else in the created order as they have free will. Everything can suffer an evil by being caused to fall short of what it should be but only angels and human beings can freely choose to be less than they are intended to be. They have been given FREEDOM and this freedom can be misused. It is the misuse of freedom that gives rise to moral evil and it is this that the Adam and Eve story explores.

So a human being can fall short of what it is to be a full human being in two ways:

1. *He or she can suffer a physical defect, or*

2. *He or she can voluntarily choose to be morally less than God intended human beings to be.*

Moral evil, therefore, occurs when humans used their freedom to fall short of God's intention for them. This is sin or moral evil – it is to do things that go against human nature. Humans are responsible for all moral evil yet St Augustine considered that these moral choices have a mysterious impact on the natural world and bring about natural evil as well. Augustine therefore brilliantly explained the existence of evil not in terms of a power or an independent principle in the world, but as an absence of good. The source of evil is human and angelic free choice, which has an impact on the natural world to make it fall short of perfection too.

ST THOMAS AQUINAS

St Thomas Aquinas was also a brilliant philosopher and theologian. Sadly he is not studied in many philosophy courses today, yet his thought lies beneath the whole of the Catholic understanding of ethics and it underpins the Natural Law tradition. Aquinas used the philosophy of Aristotle to explain how God can be talked about and also how morality should be understood. Aquinas followed Augustine's understanding of evil (which was also based on Aristotle) but he made a number of significant changes.

St Augustine accepted the Biblical account of creation and understood it to mean that in the beginning God created the world with no natural evil – no volcanoes, no earthquakes and no disease. All these natural evils were introduced as a result of the rebellion of humans and the angels against God. Aquinas, however, found this explanation for natural evil unconvincing. He said that God made lions so that they killed deer and other animals, God made volcanoes and earthquakes so that they behaved as they should do. These things, he said, were good because they fulfilled their nature. Indeed anything that fulfilled its nature was to that extent good. A volcano that erupts is a good volcano, a dingo that eats a sheep is a good dingo – they are good because they are doing what they are designed or intended to do. They are fulfilling their nature. Certainly if a sheep is eaten by a dingo then from the sheep's point of view this is a bad thing, but from the dingo's viewpoint the dingo is fulfilling its nature. If people are killed by a volcano because they build houses close by then it is undoubtedly bad for the people, but the volcano is being a good volcano because it is doing what volcanoes are intended to do – relieve pressure from under the earth's crust.

Take the example of a cat playing with a mouse. Cats appear to be quite cruel as they "play" with mice they have caught before killing them. If you were a mouse you would undoubtedly think that the cat was bad, but the cat is fulfilling its nature – it is doing what cats are meant to do. It is, therefore, a good cat. Similarly an AIDS virus is a good AIDS virus if it does what it is intended to do – but to the person who is dying of AIDS then clearly the virus appears to be a bad thing.

Aquinas, then, looks at the problem of evil from God's perspective. From this perspective, anything that fulfills its nature is good. The world was created perfect but that, for Aquinas, does not mean that it was created any differently from the way it is now. This is the best possible world and it is the world God created. Effectively Aquinas denies that natural evil exists. However Aquinas agreed with Augustine that evil should be defined as a privation, where a thing does not fulfill its nature. In particular, moral evil occurs where a person uses their free will to fall short of what God has intended them to be. There is, then, no evil power independent of God – even the devil is regarded as an angel who has fallen short of his angelic nature. For further discussion on this see the chapter on Satan.

QUESTIONS FOR CONSIDERATION

1. If God knew the damage that giving the first human beings the chance to disobey him would cause, was God right to take the risk?

2. Is evil a positive, independent force that acts in the world, or is evil simply something that human beings (and perhaps angels) create – as maintained by the stories in Genesis. Many modern films and books do consider that there actually is an evil force that acts in the world and that this force is not dependent on God.

3. In many countries in sub-Sahara Africa the rate of AIDS amongst newborn babies is sometimes as high as 25%. Aquinas would say that an AIDS virus is a good virus as it is fulfilling its nature and doing what it is intended to do. If God created the nature of all things, what questions does this raise?

4. If Aquinas is right and this is the world that God created and that the AIDS virus is a good virus and a volcano that erupts and kills peoples is a good volcano, could God not have done a better job of creation to reduce the amount of suffering in the world?

EVIL RELATED
TO FREEDOM
AND LOVE

S t Augustine and St Thomas Aquinas attempted to show that ultimately evil is not caused by God. This depends on the claim that
God chose to create creatures with free will. Allowing free will
meant that humans had, and have, the genuine option of evil rather than
good. Evil is permitted by God as the predictable consequence of free
will, but not created by Him. God does not act to counter evil when it
happens because it is not a "something" but rather a "nothing" – an
absence of good. God is not the source of natural and moral evil; the disobedience of humans (and in some traditions the disobedience of the
angels) is to blame. This explanation for the source of evil, based on
Genesis stories of creation, has dominated Christian thinking for many
centuries. Negative attitudes towards women and the natural order are
rooted in this myth. However, there is another tradition within
Christianity that suggests that evil is in fact created by God, and that evil
presents humans with an opportunity.

John Hick, a modern British philosopher has developed this tradition that
finds its origins in Bishop Irenaeus (120-202 BCE). Hick rejects the traditional approach to the source of evil offered by Augustine and Aquinas claiming
that it lacks plausibility. **Hick maintains that the idea of humans having**

John Hick rejects the Adam and Eve story

been created perfect in the Garden of Eden and then having fallen from grace is not convincing. Scientific knowledge indicates that humanity has been in an evolutionary process of growth over hundreds of thousands of years. There never was a time when mankind was morally perfect; rather humanity has emerged from lower life forms. All the evidence indicates that mankind has **developed** morally and spiritually. In addition there is evidence that there were earthquakes, dinosaurs and countless other creatures long before human beings evolved on the planet, so human moral evil cannot be an explanation for natural evil. Human beings have had to struggle throughout history and this world is a place where there is not only a physical struggle to master the environment but also a spiritual struggle. The approach of St Augustine and St Thomas Aquinas, says Hick, is part of a "pre-scientific world-view" (John Hick, *Encountering* Evil, p 40-41). It no longer seems plausible and Christianity has to provide a better explanation for the existence of evil than one rooted in a Biblical myth.

TWO FOLD STAGE OF CREATION

John Hick finds his inspiration in St Irenaeus who was bishop of Lyons in France. St Irenaeus was one of the very earliest Christian theologians and wrote well before Augustine. The Irenaean framework does not use the Genesis story of Adam and Eve's disobedience as a way of explaining the origin of evil, but instead focuses on one single verse from the first account of creation: Genesis 1:26

"Then God said, let us make man in our image, after our likeness."

From this verse Irenaeus concluded that there were two stages of creation. This is undoubtedly a curious reading of the text, but Irenaeus understood it to mean that humans were created in the image of God – as personal and moral beings, but that they had to grow into the likeness of God. By this "likeness" Irenaeus meant that humans are born with the potential for moral and spiritual growth but achieving the "likeness" of God is a person's life work. It means achieving a quality in human life that reflects the divine life.

Blake's picture of the creation of Adam is an image that captures this idea of a two-stage creation very well. In Blake's painting, Adam, as part of creation is encircled by the serpent. This is a symbol for evil and sin. Adam lies in the mud although created by God and is not able to look at God. The similarity in appearance between God and Adam is certainly there, but this Adam is not created absolutely perfect. He is trapped by the snake and his life work is to grow into the likeness of God. He has the potential to develop spiritually into the likeness of God and to grow morally, but this will be a long and arduous process. Irenaeus, Hick and Blake are all exploring the way that in life humans do not experience an automatic relationship with God yet automatically find

William Blake. Elohim creating Adam

doing the wrong thing very easy indeed. By contrast with Augustine and the more popular Christian view about evil, this idea is saying that this is the way God created people. There was never a time when all was perfect. This is the way it is and this is the way it has always been. God created evil and created us in the midst of it. The source of evil is God.

So, whereas for St Augustine the source of evil was in the free choice of Adam and Eve to be disobedient, for John Hick and Irenaeus it is part of the creative work of God. The source of evil is God. Every human being has the freedom to stay like this and to refuse to move from this first stage of creation in which they are really no more than an animal, or to begin the task of creating themselves into the likeness of God by recognizing themselves as a spiritual creature, made by God. Humans are capable of becoming like God but it is easier to choose to remain in an animal state, responding to desires and instincts and harbouring thoughts such as "Well, I'm only human".

This understanding about creation claims that this is far from the truth. Every person can grow into a human being who is able to show love, compassion, gentleness and goodness but this depends on their free choice. In the books about Harry Potter and Frodo Baggins these characters are the sort of characters they are because they make the more difficult choices in life – as Dumbledore tells Harry Potter: "It is not our gifts and abilities that make us who we are, but our choices". People have the freedom to choose what they wish to become. According to Irenaeus, human beings are created in the image of God but this is only the raw material and they have to make choices to become creatures of love who are like God in their ability to be compassionate, gentle and good. The features of this "likeness" are revealed in the person of Christ and the process of man's creation is the work of the Holy Spirit. In 2 Corinthians 3:18 St Paul writes of how humanity changes into the likeness of God:

"And we all, with unveiled faces beholding the glory of the lord are being changed into his likeness from one degree of glory to another: for this comes from the lord who is the spirit."

The evil that God provides in the world is a gift. It is a gift that is given to facilitate human growth FROM BEING IN THE IMAGE TO GROWING INTO THE LIKENESS OF GOD.`

William Blake. Jacob's Ladder (1805)

The world is a place to grow, mature and develop. Creation of human beings is the result of a long evolutionary process during which we have developed into intelligent ethical and religious animals. This approach, therefore, takes evolution seriously and recognizes that God works through evolution to bring God's purposes about. There never was a time of perfection; Adam and Eve are part of a myth. Life on this planet has always been a struggle. The struggle is not only a physical one of survival but also a spiritual one.

In the picture of Jacob's dream of a ladder ascending to heaven the idea of life as a journey to God is depicted. Human beings can embark on the journey and start the climb towards God by becoming people who practice the virtues and show compassion and love or they can choose to reject the challenge and instead be content with their lower, merely human nature.

The fall, for Augustine, happened in the Garden of Eden, when Eve took the fruit from the tree of knowledge, but for Irenaeus the fall happens when human beings through their free choice refuse to move from the animal to the spiritual. This movement into the likeness of God is also recorded in John's Gospel as people are challenged, through faith in Jesus, to move from animal life to eternal life.

THE EPISTEMIC DISTANCE

John Hick has developed this approach to evil in an attempt to show that the presence of evil does not make belief in an all loving, all powerful, good God irrational.

"Those who have some degree of Christian faith should not abandon it in the face of evil, nor should those who lack Christian faith rule it out on this account as a possibility for themselves."

"The aim of a Christian theodicy must be the relatively modest and defensive

one of showing that the mystery of evil does not render irrational a faith that has arisen, not from the inferences of natural theology, but from participation in a stream of religious experience which is continuous with that recorded in the Bible."

The question remains why God should create a world and leave no sign of himself in it. Why go to all this trouble and then leave your creation to flounder in the dust looking for you? Hick claims that the reason God is not clearly evident in the world is to protect human free choice. If the purpose of human life is to grow into the knowledge and likeness of God, and this must be done as a matter of free choice, then God making himself obvious in the world would counter this. If the existence of God were obvious then humans would be less free in their choices. For humans to have true complete freedom, God must hold himself at a distance. The reason for this is that if humans dwelt directly in God's presence their freedom would disappear. This distance, Hick calls an epistemic distance (which means a distance in knowledge terms) and God creates humans at a distance from God's self in order to preserve freedom.

The world, Hick argues, is religiously ambiguous. This means that the world can be interpreted as the creative work of God OR as a secular entity. There is nothing obvious about God's presence on this planet. It could be that we are just a part of a random solar system in a random universe. This is perfectly possible. Equally it is possible that the world and all things in it are the creative work of God. The epistemic distance is maintained so that this tension exists. The world is created as an autonomous system and it can appear as if there is no God. This leaves individuals free to accept God or to reject Him and this freedom, Hick

William Blake. Adam before God (1795)

Suffering

• Psalm 199 v 71 says "It is good for me to have been in trouble so that I could learn your laws". Many people find God through suffering. When their lives are happy and successful, God seems irrelevant but when trouble (eg severe illness or injury, persecution, natural disasters, etc) comes then suddenly there is a need for prayer and a recognition that a life lived without God is empty. Suffering, therefore, can be a route to bring people closer to God.

• C S Lewis expressed this well in "The Problem of Pain" when he said that pain and suffering are the means God sometimes uses to bring people closer to God.

• Jesus continually told His disciples that those who followed him would face persecution, loss of family and even death – yet they were meant to rejoice when this happened because these could be marks that they were taking the journey to God seriously.

argues, is essential if human beings are to develop into creatures of love and compassion.

If God were an obvious presence in the world humans could not come to know and love Him by free choice because they would already know and love him, being in His glorious presence. Human life would thus have no purpose. So, on this approach, the purpose of human life is so that individuals can come to knowledge and love of God. Given this assumption, then God has to create human at a distance from Himself to preserve their freedom.

Blake's painting (previous page) of God judging Adam shows Adam looking down on the ground. God has Adam constantly in His sight but Adam cannot see God. We, according to the Irenean tradition, are like this – we are created at a distance from God and have to journey towards God through faith.

William Blake. Nebuchadnezzar (1795)

Human beings are, therefore, born in sin and continue in this state until they choose otherwise.

On this approach, the Harry Potters, Luke Skywalkers and Frodo Baggins of this world achieve their goodness as a result of a hard won struggle, in a world that is religiously ambiguous. Love, compassion and the like can be achieved by all human beings but the freedom that makes this possible can also turn to evil. We all have to make choices and to "create ourselves", but this is only possible because of the freedom that God allows and God can only make this freedom possible if there is no obvious sign that God exists.

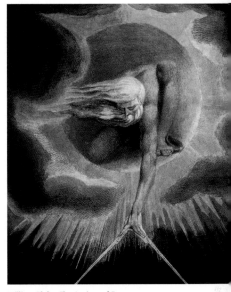

William Blake. The Ancient of Days

Human beings have a choice as to what to become. They can move from being made in the image of God to being made in the likeness of God, or they can instead go in the opposite direction and become like animals – using their freedom to be selfish, to act according to their instincts and desires. This is well portrayed in William Blake's picture of Nebuchadnezzar who was cursed by God and became like an animal eating grass.

"At once this was fulfilled. Nebuchadnezzar was cast out from among men, he ate grass like an ox, and his body was bathed with the dew of heaven, until his hair grew like the feathers of an eagle, and his nails like the claws of a bird." (Daniel 4:30)

God, therefore, uses evil as a means to bring about the highest good. This is not the best possible world but, John Hick claims, it is the best possible way for us to arrive at the best possible world – which he considers to be heaven. Hick is a "universalist", he maintains that everyone will eventually achieve salvation and get to heaven. He sees human beings as being on a journey towards God – but this means us turning ourselves into creatures of love and compassion. This world is a "vale of soul making" – a place where human beings gradually move towards being like God. **Evil and suffering, for Hick, is positive not negative. Through suffering individuals are made aware of the need for God and can grow spiritually to be closer to God.**

Hick does not emphasize the importance of reason alone – he writes from a Christian perspective, which assumes the existence of God and also assumes that love is the most important thing in the universe. The task of human beings is to develop into creatures who can show love and when we do this we will become like God. In two paintings by Blake we see God, in a painting sometimes referred to as "The Ancient of Days"(previous page) and Newton at the bottom of the sea (opposite). Blake was making a critical point about the limits of reason in each of these paintings, but even so God and Newton have one thing in common – they both have the ability to create. The pair of dividers is a symbol of rationality but also of creativity. Even though Blake was a bitter critic of Newton, who emphasized the rationality of the laws of nature, Newton as a human being has freedom and the capacity to use this freedom to move from being in the image of God to the likeness of God. He can choose to stick with reason alone and look at the floor, but he has the potential for so much more than this. He can grow into the likeness of God. Evil and suffering, the cold hard seat of the ocean bed that Newton appears to be sitting on, are all opportunities for human growth. The world is created as a place of suffering and evil in order that it can be a VALE OF SOUL MAKING. If the world were a place where no evil or suffering happened then there would be no opportunities to grow, and that, for Hick, is why we are here. Evil has a positive role, a positive value and God creates it deliberately for human benefit.

This child was born on the streets of Guatemala. He has no father, his mother is a drug addict and he lives with other street children by begging and stealing. Nobody would notice if he disappeared, and many street children in Guatemala "just disappear". He does not go to school and has few opportunities. John Hick assumes that the suffering of such children is justified by the moral and spiritual growth that the suffering will bring to them. How convincing is this?

This approach, relies on three major assumptions:

1. That God exists. God is not evident in the world and the idea of an epistemic gap may just be a way of hiding from the fact that God does not exist. This explanation for the source of evil depends on the belief that God exists and that he created and sustains the world.

William Blake. Newton at the bottom of the sea

2. That the purpose of existence is for human beings to grow into being people of love and compassion. How do we know this?

3. That human beings are free to choose the kind of people they become. We would all like to assume that we are free to make choices, but the more we learn about genetics and the way we are educated from a very young baby, the more it may be argued that we are not free but determined (see Chapter 11).

Hick accepts that the first two statements cannot be proved – they are faith statements. Nevertheless he maintains that they are reasonable and the existence of evil in no way counters these faith claims. God has good reason to allow evil in order to achieve God's purposes and without suffering and pain we could not develop into people made for a love relationship with God.

This approach to the source of evil finds the source in God. God creates evil for the greater good. As a parent might punish a child to help them learn so God gives evil to help people to grow.

QUESTIONS FOR CONSIDERATION

1) Do people mature and develop in wisdom and goodness as they experience evil and suffering?

2) What does it mean to say that the world is "religiously ambiguous" and is this true?

3) John Hick assumes that everyone will reach salvation eventually. This justifies the amount of evil and suffering in the world. What are the strengths and weaknesses of this position?

4) People sometimes freely choose to do the wrong thing. Couldn't God have created human beings so that they always freely choose to do the right thing? If God could have done this, then surely God should have done this in order to reduce the amount of suffering in the world. If God could do this and did not, then does this means that God is not good and is therefore not worthy of worship?

5) What would a world with no suffering and evil actually be like?

SATAN OR THE DEVIL

In films such as *The Exorcist* and *The Advocate* the devil is the force that is active against all forces of good. The archetypal image of the devil pictures him with a sinister smile, dressed in black or red, with horns and a tail, carrying a three-pronged triad. The triad is a reminder that the devil's realm is in hell where the living flesh of those who go there is roasted over open flames. The triad is used to spike the roasting person so that they can be turned over. The cooked flesh heals and re-grows ready to be roasted anew. We owe much to this modern day picture of the devil and hell to Dante's *Inferno* but during the medieval period gruesome paintings of what the unfaithful could expect were very common and pictured hell in similar terms.

In the painting by William Blake of the archangel Michael binding Satan the gruesome nature of the devil is portrayed. In some books and paintings (such as the one by Goya entitled "The Great He-Goat and Witches Sabbat") the devil is portrayed as a horned goat and witches surround him in secret covens. Women were burnt as witches in the middle ages sometimes because they had the "devil's mark" on them (which was basically a spot where they could not feel pain) or else just because they were old and "different". Literature has also contributed to this impression of the power of the devil and hell with plays, such as *Dr Faustus*, perpetuating the idea of grim punishment for those who play the devil's game. It is somewhat surprising, given these long color-ful traditions, to learn that in some ancient traditions the devil was not regarded as "evil" at all. This chapter will trace various traditions about the devil and will explore how some of the world's religions have regarded Satan or the devil.

THE JEWISH TRADITION

In Judaism the same God who creates good creates evil. God is entirely responsible for both. In Isaiah 45:7, the prophet describes God's creation plan when he records God as saying:

"I form the light, and create darkness; I make peace, and create evil; I the Lord do all these things."

And in the book of Lamentations:

"Who has commanded and it came to pass, unless the Lord has ordained it? Is it not from the mouth of the Most High that good and evil come?" (Lamentations 3:37-8)

William Blake. St Michael binding Satan

God creates good and evil and is responsible for good and evil in the world. Natural evils, such as volcanoes or tornadoes, are all created by God and the potential for moral evil in humans is also his creation. It is for humans to decide whether to use their freedom of choice to bring moral evil into reality. For instance:

"Here, then, I have today set before you life and prosperity, death and doom. If you obey the commandments of the LORD, your God, which I enjoin on you today, loving him, and walking in his ways, and keeping his commandments, statutes and decrees, you will live and grow numerous, and the LORD, your God, will bless you in the land you are entering to occupy. If, however, you turn away your hearts and will not listen, but are led astray and adore and serve other gods then..." (Deuteronomy 30:15-17)

Moses confronts the people of Israel with a choice – they can either choose good or evil and must take the consequences:

A common Jewish toast is "to life" – this is an affirmation of the choice of goodness rather than evil. Both are present in creation by the direct command of God. This choice, to side with life and goodness, is the choice to live in obedience to God. Any other choice is a choice to live in the absence of God.

Within this framework the Jewish scriptures do not see the devil or Satan as an independent force of evil, still less a being outside of God's created order. In the Hebrew Scriptures Satan is an agent of God. He is a servant of God faithfully carrying out the will of God as he does in all his tasks. Satan is among a whole series of angels referred to in the Hebrew Scriptures. The Hebrew word for angel is malach, meaning "messenger" and the English word angel, comes from the Greek angelos which also means "messenger". An angel is a messenger of God who carries out the divine will of God and this applies to Satan, in Hebrew Scriptures, as much as to any other angel. There is not one single example in the Jewish scriptures where any angel, Satan included, opposes God's will and for Jewish scholars it would have been unthinkable that any angelic being could have rebelled against the will of God.

William Blake. Job's son and daughters are destroyed

The role of Satan as a messenger from God is clearest in the biblical Book of Job. In the story of Job Satan appears with the other angels before God and suggests that God should test Job's loyalty to Him. God agrees to this test and Satan, as God's messenger, removed from Job all material possessions including all of his sons and daughters. In the face of all this, Job remains faithful. Satan suggests to God that the test should be made more severe. He asks God for permission to cover Job with boils so that he cannot even sit down in comfort. Again God agrees and again Satan acts only as a messenger with the permission of and on behalf of God.

Job, having lost everything and now being covered in boils, cannot understand what is happening to him. He questions why God created him and, in his despair, he wishes that he had died in his mother's womb. However after going through a long programme of anger against God, Job's faith and trust in God is vindicated. The test, given to Job by Satan with God's permission, turns out to have been the means used by God to deepen Job's faith (for a more detailed treatment of the Book of Job, see Chapter Nine).

In a second example from the Hebrew Scriptures, Numbers 22, God sends Satan, his messenger, to stand in the way of the prophet Balaam as he sets out on a journey. However Satan is invisible and only Balaam's ass can see him. The ass refuses to go on so Balaam beats the ass. The ass will not move past Satan but Balaam cannot understand why. Eventually God causes the ass to speak to Balaam and only then is Balaam allowed to see Satan, the messenger of God, and turns back (notice Satan is portrayed as an angel in white as befits God's messenger). It is interesting that many Christian bibles translate Satan as "an angel" but in Judaism it is very clear that Satan is one of the messengers of God and, as in the Book of Job, Satan only acts on God's authority. He does not have any evil power and nor does he have an evil inclination.

Satan invisible to Balaam stands before him

The Christian translators of the Hebrew Scriptures did not want to portray God as creating evil, so in some translations they altered the meaning of Isaiah's words in, for instance, the New International version of the Bible as they translate the Hebrew word rah as "disaster" instead of correctly translating it as "bad" or "evil". The NIV Bible therefore mistranslates Isaiah 45:7 to read:

"I form the light and create darkness, I bring prosperity and create disaster; I, the Lord, do all these things."

The word "disaster" is unclear and an ill–informed reader could take it to refer to natural disasters such as volcanoes and tidal waves but this was not Isaiah's message. The correct translation is:

"I form the light, and create darkness; I make peace, and create evil; I the Lord do all these things."

ZOROASTRIANISM

Zoroastrianism is a religion in which the devil has played a very significant role as a power of evil (see Ch.2). Zoroastrianism continues as a very small religion to the present day under the name of Parsiism. The whole of Zoroastrianism is structured around the dualism of good and evil. The devil is the personification of the force of evil.

FROM SATAN THE MESSENGER TO SATAN THE DEVIL

By the time the Christian Scriptures were written there is an assumed knowledge about the devil/Satan. Belief about life after death, and the afterlife as a time for reward or punishment was accepted by many. Christianity has its roots in Judaism; Jesus was a Jew, so where did this understanding about evil and the devil come from? This is much speculated over.

It is possible that when the Jewish people lived under Persian rule (536-331 BCE), where Zoroastrianism was a significant influence, that ideas about the devil or Satan as a malevolent force seeped into Jewish thinking. Later, when the Jewish people were under the Seleucids further development in thinking came as a result of the terrible persecutions under Antiochus Epiphanes. This is recorded in the book of Daniel and in I and II Maccabees. In Daniel 12:2-3 there is one of the very few passages in the Hebrew Scriptures that expresses belief in the resurrection.

"And many of them that sleep in the dust of the earth shall awake, some to everlasting life and some to shame and everlasting contempt."

Ideas about heaven and hell, God and the Devil are not well developed, but it is

possible that the seeds for these ideas are planted here. Many Jewish thinkers, like the Sadducees in the time of Jesus, did not accept belief in life after death, heaven and hell, or angels, but these ideas were clearly around and being discussed.

> 1 Peter 5:8 Be sober and vigilant. Your opponent the devil is prowling around like a roaring lion looking for (someone) to devour.
>
> 1 John 3:8 Whoever sins belongs to the devil, because the devil has sinned from the beginning. Indeed, the Son of God was revealed to destroy the works of the devil.

THE DEVIL OR SATAN IN CHRISTIAN SCRIPTURES

The Gospel tradition includes many references to the devil. It records Jesus as being tempted by the devil to use his powers wrongly. The devil is seen as a personal being with very great power: he claims to have power over all the kingdoms of the earth. The devil is the "father of lies" who does not even know what truth means. It was the devil that caused Judas to betray Jesus. Disease and illness is also seen as being caused by demons, which Jesus drives out. One of the most vivid of these portrayals is when Jesus drives 70 demons out of a man into a herd of pigs – the demons cause the pigs to run over a cliff and kill themselves. In this painting Satan is shown being driven over the cliff by Jesus. Satan is the symbol for all the demons vanquished by Jesus' action. In many of the miracles of healing that Jesus does it is clear that it was not just disease that was being sent out of the person, but Satan himself.

The devil being driven off a cliff by Jesus

Light and Darkness

The Christian Gospels do not concentrate on heaven and hell but give far more attention to the contrast between light and darkness. Those who are evil have chosen darkness for themselves – they are exiled from the light provided by Jesus and this is a consequence of their actions. The devil is portrayed as the father of lies and the source of darkness.

Matthew 8:12 ... but the children of the kingdom will be driven out into the outer darkness, where there will be wailing and grinding of teeth.

Matthew 22:13 Then the king said to his attendants, "Bind his hands and feet, and cast him into the darkness outside."

Matthew 25:30 And throw this useless servant into the darkness outside.

Luke 1:79 ... to shine on those who sit in darkness and death's shadow, to guide our feet into the path of peace.

Luke 11:34 The lamp of the body is your eye. When your eye is sound, then your whole body is filled with light, but when it is bad, then your body is in darkness.

Luke 11:35 Take care, then, that the light in you not become darkness.

Luke 11:36 If your whole body is full of light, and no part of it is in darkness, then it will be as full of light as a lamp illuminating you with its brightness.

Luke 22:53 Day after day I was with you in the temple area, and you did not seize me; but this is your hour, the time for the power of darkness.

John 1:5 ... the light shines in the darkness, and the darkness has not overcome it.

John 3:19 And this is the verdict, that the light came into the world, but people preferred darkness to light, because their works were evil.

John 8:12 Jesus spoke to them again, saying, "I am the light of the world. Whoever follows me will not walk in darkness, but will have the light of life."

John 12:35 Jesus said to them, "The light will be among you only a little while. Walk while you have the light, so that darkness may not overcome you."

John 12:46 I came into the world as light, so that everyone who believes in me might not remain in darkness.

In the letters written by Christian leaders soon after Jesus' death the devil is again portrayed in personal terms – all who do evil belong to the devil.

With this background, it is not easy to claim that the devil is irrelevant to Christianity and in western European culture the devil has been and remains a powerful image albeit one to which fewer and fewer theologians or priests make any reference.

DEVELOPING IDEAS ABOUT THE DEVIL/SATAN IN CHRISTIANITY

Many Christians are unhappy with the picture of the devil/Satan in the gospel tradition. If this is a true picture of the world then it means that God did not create everything – the devil is an independent force, out of God's control. It means a significant limit is placed on the power of God, so that he cannot easily control illness and disease, for example. Christianity believes that God created the world out of nothing and is the source of all that is. How can this belief be squared with belief in the devil and a power of evil in the world? Christianity is unique in that the triumph of God over evil, whatever the source of that evil, is seen to reside in weakness. Christianity is a religion based on historical events and it was the historical events of the life and death of Jesus, the incarnate son of God, that marks the triumph of good over evil. In particular the crucifixion, which was a Roman death penalty designed to humiliate and drag out the death of wrong doers, is believed to be the moment of ultimate triumph over evil. In

Simon Vouet. The devil conquered by Love, Beauty and Hope. (1646)

Christianity it is this moment of history when humiliation and weakness finally triumph over evil. Some Christian painters and theologians have symbolized this with images of the power of the devil eventually being defeated by truth, love and beauty. Indeed the power of these three are generally held to be irresistible (the painting is by Simon Vouet – "Satan being killed by Love, Beauty and Hope" painted in 1646). **Christianity has always held that God's power is shown in weakness not in strength.** The Book of Revelations pictures St Michael and his angels riding out to do battle against the devil and his angels – but the outcome of the battle is unquestioned.

The tension between God as all-powerful and creator of all, and the existence of an independent force of evil was not really addressed successfully until the time of Augustine, and his logic was worked on further by Aquinas.

St Augustine and St Thomas Aquinas

Some people have sought to solve the dilemma outlined above by suggesting that the devil is just a symbol for the inclination that people feel to do wicked things. This theory would suggest that the devil does not exist, except in the human mind. People do not want to take responsibility for their bad behaviour and so invent the "devil" as a way of avoiding blame themselves. A major challenge to this is the counter suggestion that if we can explain the devil in these terms – as an invention of the human mind to explain wicked inclinations – then why not explain God in the same way? On this view God does not really exist, but is just a symbol to explain the remarkable goodness that individuals are capable of doing. Others seek to undermine the gospel tradition by showing that there are differences between the gospel accounts – St John in particular resists any suggestion of a force independent of God in the world. There is, however a strong gospel tradition about the devil and it is this that St Augustine takes seriously in his approach to the devil.

The angel, Lucifer, rebels against God and becomes the devil

In the earlier chapter on the source of evil we saw that St Augustine worked with the philosophy of Aristotle to explain the existence of evil as an absence of good. Working within the gospel tradition about the devil, Augustine uses this same logic to explain the existence of the devil or Satan. He argues that Satan really exists but that his existence and his evil power is nothing more than an absence of good. Evil is to be found, for Augustine, in a falling short of something from its God-given nature. Logically therefore the devil must have fallen short from his God-given nature. Originally in the Hebrew Scriptures Satan is seen as a member of God's court who acts as a messenger – this means **that the devil was originally an angel.** The devil exits as a wicked force and tempts people away from God. Augustine was in no doubt about the power of the devil but understood the devil to be a rebellious angel. There is no justification for this in Hebrew or Christian scriptures but what Augustine does is to offer a rational explanation for the experience people have of evil, and the devil, AND the experience Christians have of an all powerful, good creator God. Augustine's theology leaves us with no logical contradiction between these two claims. The devil, for Augustine, is not an equal to God but an angel who used free will to rebel against God. The devil, therefore, was **a fallen angel** who fell short of what it was to be an angel by an act of rebellion against God. The devil is still a dependent creature – created and kept in existence by God, but he has become full of pride and his rebellion against God is an act of sin. The only part of the Scriptures that can be used to support this position of the devil as a fallen angel is in Isaiah 14:12, which says:

"How have you fallen from the heavens, O morning star, son of the dawn!
How are you cut down to the ground, you who mowed down the nations!"

The Latin Bible, the Vulgate, translated "morning star" as "the devil" as Christian writers wished to see this as a foretelling of the destruction of the devil, but this is probably a mistranslation of the Hebrew and commentators claim that in its original context the expression "morning star" refers to the King of Babylon.

For Augustine there is no independent force of evil in the world, he was certainly not a dualist. Everything that exists is part of God's creation and everything is good in that it exists. **According to Augustine and Aquinas the devil was a created, dependent being** – an angel made to dwell in the presence of God. But the devil rebelled against God and is evil to the extent that the devil has rebelled against God. This view was important for the early Church Fathers who wished to see Jesus as overturning the power of the devil. St Augustine and St Thomas Aquinas saw the Devil as good insofar as the devil fulfilled the nature of an angel (and he did this by existing) but evil insofar as he fell short of what God intended him to be – an angel. The devil is good, then, in that he exists but evil in that he rebelled against God. The devil is therefore a dependent creature of God, just as everything else in the universe depends on God.

This understanding of the devil has been used as a way of understanding the story of the Garden of Eden. The poet John Milton following in Augustine's footsteps wrote an epic poem, *Paradise Lost*. In this poem Satan seeks retaliation for having been thrown out of God's court and sees the perversion of the perfect world that God has created as a way of having his revenge. In the poem he transfigures himself into the serpent and whispers into the ear of Eve to take the forbidden fruit. Although still ultimately dependent on God for his existence, the devil tempts people away from their God-given nature so that they too will fall short. To the extent that they fall short they become evil. It is possible for humans to fall short a very long way indeed, so that they appear to be totally evil, but the Christian tradition maintains that there is always a way back to God. The reason for this is two fold:

1. *Because the work of Jesus on the cross guarantees forgiveness for those who repent.*

2. *Because the power of the devil is limited. It is limited because he is a creature of God, and ultimately dependent on God. This means that truth and goodness are stronger than evil and lies. It also means that humans, if they ask for divine assistance can, with the grace of God (which was won for all people for all time by Jesus), always resist temptation.*

St Augustine tells the story of creation when all the angels were created perfectly good. Like humans the angels were given free will. Some angels chose to turn away from God by the exercise of their free will. The Dominicans and the Franciscans were later to differ as to why the demons rebelled against God – the two alternatives being that either they rebelled due to pride or due to having too high an opinion of their own excellence. It was this rebellion, however caused, which turned angels into demons. It is arrogance or pride that is held to have caused the devil to fall from heaven to hell. Confidence in self and pride in his own abilities as a power independent of God are the key factors that make the devil what he is.

The devil and demons continue to act as they do with God's permission and God sustains and keeps them in existence. God uses the devil as a way of punishing people even though, according to Augustine, the devil is often not aware of this. In the last analysis, however, the devil and the demons will be condemned to permanent hell and this Augustine sees as a fulfillment of God's plans and another indication of God's glory.

Today, the idea of God deciding that even the devil and demons, still less human beings who have done wrong, should permanently be in eternal punishment without there being any possibility of reprieve is considered by many to be unacceptable. The very idea of heaven for the good and hell for the wicked is challenged by some theologians as it may be asked whether any evil is sufficient to justify everlasting punishment in hell. Rossetti's poem *The*

The Devil in the Gospels

Matthew 4:1 Then Jesus was led by the Spirit into the desert to be tempted by the devil.

Matthew 4:5 Then the devil took him to the holy city, and made him stand on the parapet of the temple.

Luke 4:3 The devil said to him, "If you are the Son of God, command this stone to become bread."

Luke 4:6 The devil said to him, "I shall give to you all this power and glory; for it has been handed over to me, and I may give it to whosoever I wish.

Matthew 4:11 Then the devil left him and, behold, angels came and ministered to him.

An antlered devil in Skulderlev church in Denmark. The devil is often portrayed in ways that are relative to the culture in which the painting is made

Matthew 13:39 and the enemy who sows them is the devil. The harvest is the end of the age, and the harvesters are angels.

Matthew 25:41 Then he will say to those on his left, "Depart from me, you accursed, into the eternal fire prepared for the devil and his angels."

Luke 8:12 Those on the path are the ones who have heard, but the devil comes and takes away the word from their hearts that they may not believe and be saved.

John 6:70 Jesus answered them, "Did I not choose you twelve? Yet is not one of you a devil?"

John 8:44 You belong to your father the devil and you willingly carry out your father's desires. He was a murderer from the beginning and does not stand in truth, because there is no truth in him. When he tells a lie, he speaks in character, because he is a liar and the father of lies.

John 13:2 The devil had already induced Judas, son of Simon the Iscariot, to hand him over.

IN EACH OF THESE EXAMPLES THE DEVIL COULD EITHER BE:

1. AN INDEPENDENT SOURCE OF EVIL

2. A FALLEN ANGEL WHO REBELLED AGAINST GOD OR

3. A CHALLENGER SENT BY GOD TO TEMPT PEOPLE OR

4. THE PERSONIFICATION OF THE EVIL PSYCHOLOGICAL INFLUENCES THAT DWELL IN THE HUMAN PSYCHE (THIS IS AN INCREASINGLY COMMON VIEW TODAY)

Blessed Damozel puts this well as it asks whether anyone could be happy in heaven if they knew that any other human being, however wicked, permanently suffered in hell. In this poem, a young girl comes to heaven and looks down from God's house to the vast realms of space below – she can barely even see the sun. Everything is there for her delight in this place of peace and joy. However she longingly looks downwards because her beloved is not with her and she knows, even though she hopes otherwise, that he is in hell and there is no prospect of their ever being together.

For a time she allows herself to imagine what it would be like if her lover comes to her, but in the end she has to face reality. There is a great gulf fixed and she will never see him again. The poem effectively asks how she can ever be happy in heaven knowing that her beloved is in hell.

The problem of hell as a place of permanent exile from God has led some modern theologians to question whether anyone at all goes to hell. They argue that hell would only be deserved by someone who:

1. *Knowingly,*

2. *Deliberately and*

3. *With full knowledge*

rejected God and, they maintain, this is not possible. Those who reject God do so because of ignorance or lack of knowledge and a compassionate and loving God would take this into account so that no one would go to hell. Also, even if hell is considered to exist, many theologians would not see it in crude terms as a place of torture but rather as a state of exile from God by those who had freely and knowingly chosen this state of exile. Whilst this is an attractive picture, it is not in accordance with traditional Christian teaching and, indeed, it seems to run directly counter to what Jesus himself said when he is recorded by the Gospel writers as graphically describing the pains of hell.

In the Middle Ages the power of the devil was unquestioned – the devil waited round every corner to tempt men and women away from righteousness. Today in Western Christianity, the devil is barely mentioned and, indeed, many priests and theologians are doubtful of the devil's existence except as a projection of the evil side of the psyche of the individual – yet the devil is a significant figure in the Christian Scriptures.

ISLAM

In Islam, Satan is called "Iblis" and is an angel, dwelling in the presence of God. When God made Adam, God commanded all the angels to do homage to Adam and to bow before Him. Iblis, however, refused. The Qu'ran says:

"And when (God) said to the angels: Make obeisance to Adam they did obeisance, but Iblis (did it not). He refused and he was proud, and he was one of the unbelievers."
(Sura 2:34)

The devotion to prayer and alms giving is a cental feature of Islam and is seen as an aid in resisting evil

Iblis refused because, as he said to God, he was better than Adam and should not bow down before him. We see here, therefore, the pride of Satan which is also a feature of Christian teaching. God commanded Iblis to go away from him and Iblis vowed as a result to tempt the sons of Adam and to lead them away from obedience to God. The Qu'ran records that God then vowed to fill hell with all those who followed Iblis. (Sura 7:18)

In Islam, Satan (Iblis) is portrayed as "the whisperer", one who whispers in the ears of men and women to persuade them away from following God. Thus when Adam and Eve are in the garden of Eden, the Qu'ran records:

"Satan (Iblis) made an evil suggestion to them that he might make manifest to them what had been hidden from them of their evil inclinations, and he said: 'Your Lord has not forbidden you this tree except that you may not both become two angels or beings that live forever.' And he swore to them both: 'Most surely I am a sincere adviser to you.'"

"Then he caused them to fall by deceit; so when they tasted of the tree, their evil inclinations became manifest to them, and they both began to cover themselves with the leaves of the garden." (Suras 20-22)

The idea of the devil as "the whisperer" is an attractive one as it portrays the devil as a persuader – but the devil does not control the individual. In Christianity and Islam, the devil tempts individuals to sin but it is the individual who makes the decision to give in to the "whispering" in his or her heart and to go along with the devil's evil promptings.

ALTERNATIVE WAYS OF UNDERSTANDING THE DEVIL

Islamic and later Christian thinking portray the devil as a created being who rebels against God. God and the devil are at enmity – the one opposes the other. However this is by no means the only understanding. There are two main alternatives to the Christian and Islamic idea:

1. *The devil as a trickster who is not evil but nasty. Loki in Norse mythology is a good example and another is in the religion of the Yoruba tribe in Africa. This includes a god named Esu who should always be worshipped ahead of the other gods (the "orisa"). If people worship him at the outset of a religious ceremony, Esu will not only be pleased, but he will also make sure that the other gods hear the person's prayers. But if people should forget to go to him first, or if they should offend him in some other way, then he might make his presence known by causing harm: making someone fall off a roof, letting a child die, and so forth. A trickster, then, is not a thoroughly evil being, just an obnoxious one who has to be dealt with very carefully because he can be extremely capricious.*

2. *The devil as one amongst a number of evil spirits that cause harm to anyone who gets in their way. These tend to be localized to a particular place and protection can be obtained often by wearing particular bracelets or other objects.*

3. *The approach in Hinduism is that there is no single god nor is there a single devil. However there are evil spirit beings and these are of two types:*

- *The mighty devil-gods, called the asuras, who have great power. In some early Hindu writings there are two kinds of divine beings: the devas ("gods") and the asuras ("lords"). These are initially neither good nor evil but as the stories about them develop there is warfare between the two groups and the devas win. As an example, the deva Indra defeats the asura Varuna.*

Increasingly the asuras come to be seen as evil, great lords who harm people and who create conflict. However this is not a hard and fast rule – the gods can do great harm (eg Kali) and the lords are not all bad.

- *The local evil spirits that dwell in homes, rice fields and forests and that are a feature of much popular Hinduism.*

In Hinduism, therefore, there is no idea of a single powerful devil – both gods and lords are powerful and both can do good as well as evil.

CONCLUSION

The idea of a force of evil has a long history and it is still relevant today. People even in the so-called educated West are still nervous of being alone in the dark and it is difficult to find anywhere that is completely dark. Most streets are lit and ambient light cannot be avoided in most Western countries. Many believe in some force of evil or dark power that is to be at least respected, treated with caution and sometimes feared. Most video stores have shelves full of films about a force of evil – vampires, trolls, demons or the like. These are not simply entertaining – they strike chords in the human mind. There are reasons for the persistence of such stories over thousands of years as they resonate with the experience, fears and beliefs of many individuals. Whether there is such a force of evil or whether talk of the devil is merely to give expression to something rooted deeply in the human mind is, of course, a real question and one which will be considered in a later chapter.

QUESTIONS FOR CONSIDERATION

1. Do you consider that there is a power of evil represented by talk of the devil or do you consider that reference to the devil is only a reference to the dark side of the human psyche?

2. If the devil is only a part of the human mind, then should God also be explained in these terms?

3. If an evil power does exist, do you consider this to be equal to God (this is a dualist position) or is it dependent on God?

4. What are the main differences between the Jewish and Christian understandings of Satan?

5. In the modern world, is talk of the devil irrelevant? If not, then why not?

CHAPTER SEVEN

CHANGING PERCEPTIONS OF GOOD AND EVIL

For nearly two thousand years "goodness" in the Western world has been regarded as being associated with and guaranteed by God and evil has been associated either with the devil or a rejection of God. God underpinned all that was good and it was generally accepted that the world was created by and depended on God.

For thousands of years God had underpinned all that was good. In the following illustration, God is the final arbiter of Beauty, Truth, Morality, Goodness and Justice. These were considered to be absolutes because they were guaranteed by God

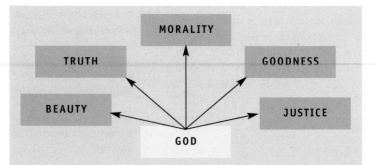

The end of the 19th century was, for much of Europe, a time of peace and prosperity. Industrialization had brought wealth to the middle classes; factories had made consumer goods available to the average person whilst railways and steamships enabled people to travel in a way never possible before. At one level this was a period of religious revival but at another level God was seen as increasingly irrelevant. Charles Darwin's discoveries of the Principle of Natural Selection, through which evolution worked, seemed to show that human beings were much like any other animal – they were not, as the Church had long held, created specifically by God and in the image and likeness of God. Instead they had evolved from other animals. There was increasing confidence in the power of the human mind to solve the problems of the world and science was advancing at a tremendous rate.

MARX AND NIETZSCHE

Into this world came two great philosophers who were both strong atheists and who were to leave legacies that had a devastating effect on the traditional values systems of the Western world – these were Karl Marx and Frederick Nietzche. Marx and Nietzche rejected God. This may not seem tremendously significant, after all there have always been people who do not believe in God. However once God is widely rejected in a society, then there is no longer any underpinning for Beauty, Truth, Morality, Goodness and Justice. Instead the only yardstick is what human beings value. Their opinion is then the only

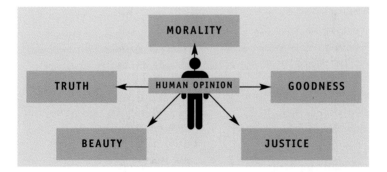

grounding for beauty, truth, morality, goodness and justice. A very different picture then emerges. Karl Marx rejected God entirely and instead considered that social change was inevitable and necessary. Religion, he argued, helped to underpin evil institutions and an unjust social order in which those with

The Madman

"Where is God gone?" he called out

"I mean to tell you!

We have killed him, you and I !

We are all his murderers!

But how have we done it?

How were we able to drink up the sea?

Who gave us the sponge to wipe away the whole horizon?

What did we do when we loosened this earth from its sun?

Whither does it now move?

Whither do we move? Away from all suns?

Do we not dash on unceasingly?

Backwards, sideways, forwards, in all directions?

Is there still an above and below?

Do we not stray, as through infinite nothingness?

Does not empty space breathe upon us?

Has it not become colder?

Does not night come on continually, darker and darker?

Shall we not have to light lanterns in the morning?

Do we not hear the noise of the grave-diggers who are burying God?

Do we not smell the divine putrefaction?

- for even Gods putrefy!

God is dead! God remains dead!

And we have killed him!

How shall we console ourselves, the most murderous of all murderers?

The holiest and the mightiest that the world has hitherto possessed, has bled to death under our knife - who will wipe the blood from us?

With what water could we cleanse ourselves?

What lustrums, what sacred games shall we have to devise?

Is not the magnitude of this deed too great for us?

Shall we not ourselves have to become Gods, merely to seem worthy of it?

There never was a greater event - and on account of it, all who are born after us belong to a higher history than any history hitherto!"

"I come too early," he then said.

"I am not yet at the right time.

This prodigious event is still on its way, and is travelling - it has not yet reached men's ears.

Lightening and thunder need time, the light of the stars needs time, deeds need time, even after they are done, to be seen and heard.

This deed is as yet further from them than the furthest star - and yet they have done it themselves!"

Friedrich Nietzsche
(1844-1900)

wealth owned the factories and companies and earned a great deal of money whilst those who worked in these factories and companies owned almost nothing at all. He saw this as exploitation and argued for communism in which the means of production (factories and farms) were owned by the State. Private enterprise and individuals seeking profit were eliminated in the interests of the greater good for workers as a whole. Marx's ideas were heavily influenced by the philosopher, Hegel, who saw an inevitability of historical forces bringing about change. Hegel was the first to write a Philosophy of History and to see how ideas developed over the centuries through a gradual process. Marx considered that these same historical forces made the fall of capitalism, monarchy and religion inevitable. These ideas were to lead to the Russian revolution in 1917, which not only overthrew the government of the Czar of Russia but also rejected religion and led to it being suppressed throughout Eastern Europe. Communism and atheism were closely aligned, communist schools suppressed any mention of religion and some people, at least, were attracted to an idea which seemed to be on the side of ordinary people in a struggle against wealth and privilege. **Evil became expressed solely in terms of sociology with no reference to any transcendent grounding for good or evil.**

Marx also rejected religion as he saw it as the enemy of social action, which was needed to remove injustice in the world. Religion, he considered, led people to quietly accept their lot in life in return for the hope of a reward after death. It was, therefore, a very effective means of social control as it kept people quiet and helped them to accept their poverty and the injustice of the social system which made them poor and kept them poor.

Nietzsche was much more an individualist than Marx but his ideas also had an enormous and possibly longer-term influence. Nietzsche rejected God – in Thus Spake Zarathustra he said that "God is dead". However by this he did not mean to simply reject the God of Christianity. Nietzsche also rejected all that God stood for and, therefore, all claims to an absolute standard of beauty, truth, goodness or evil were rejected as well. In this respect he recognized the significance of the move from Illustration 1 to Illustration 2 on pages 80 and 81. Once God is held not to exist, then all the underpinning for the old ideas of goodness and evil, morality and immorality collapse (the poem "The Madman" shows the greatness of the deed that Nietzsche considered the killing of God represented).

Nietzsche saw Christian morality, which for so long had dominated Europe, as being no more than a "herd morality". He saw Christians and Christian doctrine as pathetic and weak and, indeed, considered that it was Christian morality that had destroyed the strength and might of the Roman Empire. He admired the Romans as they were examples of a strong, self-confident people that imposed their own order on the known world. They enjoyed life and recognized the importance of power. The Empire, Nietzsche argued, was not destroyed by Barbarians fighting across its borders – it was destroyed from within by Christianity because Christianity supported all those virtues which undermined strength and power.

"Christianity was the vampire of the imperium Romanum – in a night it shattered the tremendous achievement of the Romans." (The Antichrist p.113)

Emphasis on compassion, in particular, Nietzsche completely rejected. Compassion weakened people so that they ceased to be MEN (Nietzsche's use of the male gender here is quite deliberate). Christians, he said, were encouraged to see themselves as "sinners", to be constantly seeking forgiveness, to be obedient and Nietzsche rejected all these ideas. Instead he wanted individuals to be STRONG, to stand out from the herd (the mass of ordinary people) and his ideal was the SUPERMAN who lived beyond good and evil. "Superman" here does not mean anything like the cartoon character. Instead the Superman is the one who is strong enough to see that, with the death of God, comes the death of morality. **The Superman has to be brave enough to recognize this so as to create his own values based on pride, strength and an unwillingness to accept the need for compassion for the weak – values which, in historical terms, have led to what is traditionally described as evil actions.** The picture looks something like this:

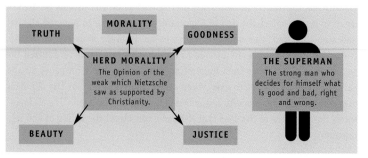

The importance of this is that Nietzsche recognizes that with the supposed death of God goes the death of all traditional morality and of any absolute difference between good and evil. All that is left is the opinion of the herd but there is no reason to follow herd morality. Instead the strong man has to recognize that he must be his own god, he must make his own decision on what is good and evil, right and wrong.

Some have said that Nietzsche was the philosopher of the Nazis as he valued strength and power, but this is to misunderstand him. He would have condemned the Nazi morality as much as any other as he wanted his Superman to stand outside any herd morality and to have the strength to be obedient only to his own vision of what was right or wrong.

POST-MODERNISM

Nietzsche was to indirectly influence post-modernism although defining post-modernism is far from easy. There is no clear moment when post-modernism began although the Paris student riots of 1968 were important. Post-modernism denies any claims to absolute truth in any sphere. There is no correct or true way of reading literature, poetry and sacred stories such as the Bible or of understanding good and evil.

Possibly the most famous definition of post-modernism is given by Jean-Francois Lyotard who says:

"I define postmodern as incredulity towards metanarratives."

A "metanarrative" is any single, grand, over-arching way of making sense of the world or claiming truth. Thus the Bible would be a metanarrative and so would science as they both give rise to general claims to truth that apply independently of time or the community that adopts them. To say that post-modernism rejects any META-NARRATIVE means that post-modernism rejects any idea of an overall way of looking at the world which is "right". There is no true story, no

Who writes history? Generally those in power, those who win the battles of history. The views of the losers or those who are marginalized such as women, the poor or social outcasts are simply ignored. History, post-modernism argues, tends to be the account gi ven of the world based on the view of those who are successful.

Epistemology

Imagine you are swimming in the middle of a raging sea. You can just about keep afloat but the sea and the tide sweep you first one way then another. You may look for some rock to cling to, some firm point onto which you can hold.

This has been the situation of humans for more than 3000 years when they have sought knowledge – they have sought to be clear on what they can and cannot know, on something stable on which their claims to know things can be founded. They have studied EPISTEMOLOGY which is the philosophy of knowledge to try to work out what can be known with certainty.

Post-modernism rejects the whole study of epistemology and argues that there are no stable and no fixed points to cling to. All there is is change and the need to live with this. The absolutes are now gone. All that remains are the different perspectives from which different people view the world. No one of these is any better or worse than any other.

idea of a true account of the world or of reality. **Truth is simply what people agree about and all absolutes are dismissed.**

Everything depends on the perspective from which individuals or groups look at issues. Thus a black, lesbian feminist will have a different understanding of truth, literature, art and morality from that of a white, heterosexual male or an aborigine. There are no absolutes and what is needed is to understand the perspectives of others, as they are neither better nor worse than yours.

As an example, the English students at Harvard University once insisted on the Boston telephone book being placed on the reading list alongside the works of Shakespeare as, according to post-modernism, there is no greater merit in the one rather than the other. **Good and evil are, therefore, totally relative to the society in which these values are held and the attempt by one society (for instance the United States, Europe and Australia/New Zealand) to impose their values on others is "cultural imperialism"** – it represents the destruction of one set of values by another and since all values are held to be equal, there is no basis for this other than an exercise in power.

Allied to post-modernism is the idea of DECONSTRUCTIONISM which seeks to determine what is NOT said in any text – for instance in an account of history to try to see whose voices have been ignored (often the voices of the poor and those of women). The French philosopher Derrida, has said "There is no meaning outside the text" – this has been taken to mean that any text has a life of its own and cannot be judged as pointing to something beyond it. All that matters is how any book (whether this be a novel or Shakespeare) is read by any particular reader. Since each reader will be different, there is then no "correct" reading of any text. Richard Rorty supports the view that by this Derrida means that the whole world we experience is just something we construct and different people therefore have different worlds. However, Derrida himself does not seem to be a "full scale" postmodernist. Immediately before saying "there is nothing outside the text" Derrida calls for a careful commentary on a text "with all the instruments of traditional criticism" to protect the meaning of the text. Otherwise interpretation of the text "... would risk developing in any direction at all and authorize itself to say almost anything." So Derrida merely seems to be saying that any text needs careful analysis – which no-one would disagree with!

My opinion is as good as anyone elses! What is true for you is not for me!

וֹד בְּמֵי מְרִיבַת מַיִם, צְמֵאִים לְהַשְׁקוֹתָם מַיִם, וְהַצְלִיחָה
: תַּעֲנֶה קְדוֹשִׁים מְנַסְּכֵים לְךָ מַיִם, וְהוֹשִׁיעָה נָּא : לְמַעַן
תוֹת מַיִם תָּלִילָה פֵּן, וְנֶסֶךְ לְךָ מַיִם, וְהַצְלִיחָה נָא
עֲנֵה שׁוֹאֲלִים בְּרְבִיעַ אֲשֶׁלֵי מַיִם, וְהוֹשִׁיעָה נָא : לַמַ
ם. תִּפְתַּח אֶרֶץ וְתַרְעֵיךְ שָׁמַיִם, וְהַצְלִיחָה נָא וְהוֹשִׁיעָ
נָא קְהַל עֲדַת יְשֻׁרוּן. סָרַח וּמָּד
הוֹשִׁיעֵנוּ אֱלֹהֵי יִשְׁעֵנוּ :
עֲבָדִים אֶל יַד אֲדוֹנִים. כָּאנוּ לְפָנֶיךָ נְדוֹנִים, וְהוֹשִׁיעֵנוּ
דוֹנֵי הָאֲדוֹנִים, נִתְגָּרוּ בָנוּ מְדָנִים, דָּשִׁנוּ וּבְעָלוּנוּ ז
אֱלֹהֵי יִשְׁעֵנוּ. הֵן בַּצְנוּ הַיּוֹם בְּתַחֲנוּן. עָרֵיךְ לֶחֶם
בְּשָׁנוּן וְהוֹשִׁיעֵנוּ אֱלֹהֵי יִשְׁעֵנוּ : זָבַת חָלָב וּדְבָשׁ.
ם בָּאֵבָה תְּחַבֵּשׁ, וְהוֹשִׁיעֵנוּ אֱלֹהֵי יִשְׁעֵנוּ : טְּעֵנוּ בְּשֶׁנֵ

Text from the Jewish scriptures

- In some Islamic countries, thieves have their hands cut off and someone caught in the act of adultery or drinking alcohol will be beaten publicly or stoned to death. In others, women who do not cover their face and arms will be beaten on the streets and put in prison.
- In some countries in West Africa, young girls of 13 are circumcised. Bribes are an essential part of everyday life.
- In some states in the US a 16-year-old-boy will be put in gaol for sleeping with his 15½ year-old girl friend.
- In the middle ages, tens of thousands of people who did not accept Church teachings were burnt to death for heresy.
- In Barbados, poor and vulnerable people are forced to swallow condoms full of cocaine and heroin to avoid customs officials in Britain and the US. After passing through customs, the drug dealers then collect the drugs.
- Money given to feed the poor often lines the pockets of the rich.
- In some countries, growing opium is legal.
- Giving the "morning after pill" to a 13-year-old-girl who has been gang raped is condemned in some societies as evil and wicked.
- In Africa, many people with AIDS believe that if they sleep with a virgin they will be cured even if the virgin is eleven years old.

DO YOU CONSIDER THAT THE RIGHTNESS OR WRONGNESS OF THESE POSITIONS SIMPLY DEPENDS ON THE SOCIETY IN WHICH ONE LIVES AND THE OPINIONS OF THOSE WITHIN THESE SOCIETIES OR DO YOU THINK THAT SOME OF THESE ARE WRONG IN AN ABSOLUTE SENSE?

Mainstream post-modernism, however, goes much further than this and claims that there is NO right reading of any text. Everything depends on the interpretation of the reader or the reading position of the person who is reading the text.

This approach, of course, emphasizes tolerance and respect for the opinion of others. **In fact TOLERANCE and RESPECT FOR THE OPINION OF OTHERS have become the new gods of Western society. All views, all moralities, all sexual orientations are to be respected.** The opinion of every person is as good as the opinion of anyone else. We see this in many classrooms where young people are asked their opinion and this is meant to be valued and respected no matter how ill-informed. So much is this so that teachers sometimes find that pupils became angry if they criticize their students' work on the grounds that every student has a right to their own opinion.

The trouble is that if "OPINION RULES OK" then no basis is left for criticizing the opinion of others when this leads to them doing terrible things. Anyone who does so can simply be accused of inflicting their own morality onto others and the claim can be made that they have no right to do so. On this basis, **good and evil become totally relative to the society in which people live and even to individual opinion.**

There is then no need to think deeply about good and evil. There is no need to analyze arguments to see if they are strong or weak, for a person to evaluate and challenge their own position or even for a person to come to recognize that their own position may be wrong. This liberal agenda, which appears so reasonable, leads to a reluctance to condemn the behaviour of any other

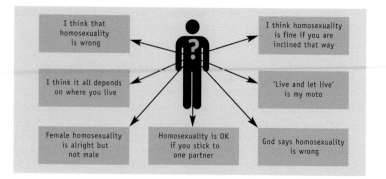

culture as WRONG when, in fact, it may be oppressive.

Replies to post-modernism have been few and far-between and the god of tolerance based on the idea that there are no absolutes still holds sway across much of Western culture. This involves a reluctance to condemn others no matter what position they hold.

There are voices that have been raised to reject post-modernism and even some philosophers who are called post-modernists reject the view that evil and good just depends on the viewpoint from which these are seen. Many seem to work with an intuition that there is more to it that this, although what grounds this intuition is sometimes far from clear. They are faced with the problem that once God is abandoned as an underpinning for good or bad, right and wrong then there seems no ways of holding onto claims to truth.

SALVADORE DALI

Salvador Dali was a surrealist. His paintings sought to express on canvas psychological insights into the nature of reality. He looked at mundane objects and events from an entirely different point of view and some have held him to be an example of a post-modern artist – yet this is very far from the truth. Dali helped develop a totally new art form which was disturbing and which challenged the status quo, yet Dali also produced some of the greatest art of the 20th century. Nietzsche's assertion that "God is dead" and his undercutting of all ideas of an absolute goodness, truth or morality might have been seen to influence Dali but in fact Nietzsche's influence went in exactly the opposite direction. In 1952, Dali recorded in his journal:

"It is true that Nietzsche, instead of driving me further into atheism, initiated me into the questions and doubts ... Nietzsche awoke in me the idea of God."

Dali sought to provide insights through his art – but he always saw his art as pointing to a religious truth. **Christianity claims that a life without God is two dimensional, like the chess board on Dali's famous painting of the cross of Jesus above the chess board of the world.** The existence of God and the struggle between good and evil makes the game of life worthwhile. Nietzsche, the atheist, was thus the cause of some of the most profound and provoking religious art ever produced and although Dali did not produce a philosophic argument to justify his claims to the mystical nature of human beings and the truths of religion, he sought to show these truths in his art. Others in this century have attempted to hold on to claims about the absolute nature of truth, morality and justice in the face of the challenge of post-modernism.

MARTIN BUBER

Martin Buber was a Jewish philosopher who attempted to wrestle with the problem of evil. He focused on the importance of seeing others as a THOU, rather than an IT. God, for Buber, was THOU – a personal reality addressed in prayer, a reality that philosophers cannot comprehend. Buber considered that, ethically, the demand is to treat others as a THOU, in other words as a full human being with rights which must be respected and recognized. For Buber evil occurs when people stop doing this – when people are treated as commodities or objects. Whenever human beings are treated as objects they are dehumanized and then it is possible to do anything to them as their humanity is then denied. Buber therefore contrasts an "I/IT" way of approaching the world and an "I/THOU" approach. Once anyone sees the face of another human being, sees them as a "Thou", as an individual, then doing evil to them becomes impossible. The task of the evildoer then is to refuse this recognition of the "Thou", to refuse to recognize the humanity of the other person. The antidote to evil according to Buber, is found in everyday life, through the creation of a community of "thous", of individuals who can be recognized and treated as neighbors. His approach is not, therefore, abstract and academic, it is essentially practical. However this position depends on Buber's faith in God and his view that every single human being is precious because he or she is a child of God. Post-modernism denies this basic premise.

Emmanuel Levinas.

EMMANUEL LEVINAS

Levinas built on Buber's insight. Levinas was profoundly influenced by the suffering and evil of the holocaust and he goes back to basic principles to try to grapple with this, He rejects the whole attempt to UNDERSTAND the problem of evil, to seek to philosophically make sense of the events of the holocaust because this implies that there is meaning and there is the possibility of understanding. Levinas simply will not accept this. Levinas rejects the philosophy of Heideggar who sought to understand what it means to BE, to exist, what it means to be human. Levinas considered that this very attempt was the culmination of the attempt by philosophy to seek to understand. People become just one more set of things within the world which the philosopher and scientist seek to understand. Levinas observes that "the best thing about philosophy is that it fails" and Levinas, as a philosopher, rejects traditional philosophy as it denies what Levinas considers to be most important. He puts it like this:

This is the century that in thirty years has known two world wars, the totalitarianisms of the right and left, Hitlerism and Stalinism, Hiroshima, the Gulag, and the genocides of Auschwitz and Cambodia. This is a century that is drawing to a close in the obsessive fear of the return of everything these barbaric names stood for: suffering and evil inflicted deliberately, but in a manner no reason has set limits to, in the exasperation of a reason become political and detached from all ethics.

Among these events the Holocaust of the Jewish people under the reign of Hitler seems to me to be the paradigm of gratuitous human suffering, in which evil appears in its diabolical horror. This is perhaps not a subjective feeling. The disproportion between suffering and every theodicy was shown at Auschwitz with a glaring obvious clarity ... Did not Nietzsche's saying about the death of God take on in the extermination camps, the meaning of a quasi-empirical fact?" (Levinas "Useless Suffering" in Entre Nous thinking-of-the-other)

What Levinas is saying here is that Nietzsche's theory of the death of God was effectively verified by the events of the 20th century (hence it is a "quasi-empirical fact"). He therefore claims that it is no longer possible to run away from the conclusions that the holocaust forces on us.

Levinas rejects the traditional view of God. He sees two irreconcilable positions:

1) *God as conceived by the philosophers and theologians and who is understood as the supreme Being, who acts in the history of the world and who is all powerful and all loving and who could have acted in the holocaust.*

Human rights or duties

Many today hold that each person has a duty to develop themselves to the full, to be what they are capable of becoming. Young people are told at school:

• Follow your dreams, and

• Make a difference

Underneath this lies the presumed right – in fact the duty – to develop themselves. Levinas rejects this understanding. Instead each person has an ethical obligation that exists NOW – at the moment when individuals confront and meet other individuals. How they respond, or fail to respond, to their neighbour determines who they are. They can walk by, ignore "the other", the person they meet, the neighbour, but if they do so they have missed an opportunity that has been given to them. They have behaved wrongly by neglect. The uniqueness of each human being lies not in our genes or in who they are, but in how they respond to the ethical challenge of meeting their neighbour. Although Levinas is Jewish there are obviously close links here with Jesus' teaching about the duty to love one's neighbour or the parable of The Good Samaritan.

According to Levinas, each human being has no rights – only duties. They have an absolute duty to "the other" and failing to recognize and act on this duty is the source of evil. **Those who emphasize their "rights" who talk about what is "due to them" or what their parents, their friends or the world owe them are dominated by ego and are in no sense ethical beings.** The alternative is to be the person who recognizes responsibilities. The ego tempts every individual to ignore duties and responsibilities in favour of developing their personality or looking after themselves. This is not necessarily bad but if it becomes the main human aim then Levinas considers that it is likely to become evil.

2) The fact that God let the Nazis do what they wanted.

Levinas cannot reconcile these two positions so he rejects the first, the traditional idea of God BUT, and this is the significant point, he does not reject what religion and above all ethics stands for and instead analyses evil in ethical terms. Levinas considers that human beings cannot be reduced to mere objects – human transcendence is experienced when we meet others. We constantly fail to see the other person as they really are. We "do violence" to them by refusing to let them be different, by refusing to recognise that they are "other". However levinas does not succeed in explaining what under-

The dehumanising effect of the death camps and slave camps of Nazi Germany

pins his ethical claims and, in the absence of god, his rejection of evil seems difficult to defend.

Whenever one human being meets another they meet their neighbour whose wish is to be seen as he or she is, to be allowed to be themselves and not to be forced to conform to the other person's view of them. All human beings tend naturally to be indifferent to others and this is the real evil that allowed the holocaust and other great suffering to take place.

Every time one person meets another there is an encounter with otherness. Effectively every person says:

"I am other to you", "I am not you."

Every person says:

"Don't judge me in your terms and by your categories. I am other than you, I am not you, I am different – allow me to be who I am rather than seeking to make me like you."

Every person, if each person will recognise it, appeals against the indifference

Christ being judged evil by religious leaders

You

- How many people REALLY know you?

- How many people see you as you really are, as opposed to seeing you in their terms?

- How often do you feel forced to pretend to be what someone else wants you to be?

- How many people do you REALLY seek to know? How often do you impose your view of who a person is, rather than respecting their difference from you?

- WE DO VIOLENCE TO OTHERS WHEN WE REFUSE TO LET THEM BE WHO THEY ARE, WHEN WE REFUSE TO ACCEPT WHO THEY ARE AND SEEK TO MOULD THEM ON OUR TERMS. This, for Levinas, is the root of evil.

of others and asks them not to be violent by judging them in their own terms. This, of course, is what those who do evil cannot see – they either cannot see or they cannot accept the difference of the other and they therefore seek to impose their own will on the other person by seeing him or her solely in their own terms. They do not look closely enough.

Levinas, therefore, accepts that the God of traditional religion who acts in the world is dead but he sees traces of God still present in the world in the ethical demands made on us by the other person that we meet. Ethics is about a one to one relationship, where one person meets another. There is a personal encounter and a challenge in every meeting. Most people refuse this challenge, they refuse to see the difference that the other person represents – they refuse to let the other person be themself and this is the origin of evil. Goodness and justice means accepting and allowing the possibility of the very real way in which every person is "other" or different to us.

THE PROBLEM

Postmodernism, following Nietzsche, rejects God or any ultimate truth. This leaves the door open for opinion to rule and for an inability to criticize the opinion of others since, it is held, the opinions of all must be respected and valued. However against this seemingly inexorable trend are those who want to hold on to an absolute idea of JUSTICE and GOODNESS as opposed to evil. The problem is how to do this philosophically once belief in God is abandoned. This is one of the central challenges for the 21st century, as without this grounding it may be that terrible evils like the holocaust are bound to re-occur.

QUESTIONS FOR CONSIDERATION

1) If God does not exist, what might underpin claims to any absolute difference between good and evil?

2) Is your opinion of what is good and evil as good as anyone else's?

3) How would you describe the strengths and weaknesses of postmodernism?

4) Is Hitler's opinion of what is good and evil as valid as that of Nelson Mandela? If not, why not?

5) Why might Nietzsche have been surprised by the effect his writings had on Salvadore Dali?

6) Buber considered that it was God that gave human beings dignity. Levinas removes a traditional understanding of God – what significance does this have for his understanding of evil?

CHAPTER EIGHT

THE FINAL SOLUTION

The TREATY OF VERSAILLES in 1919 brought an end to the First World War but it was an unfair treaty. The winners of the war, the US, Britain and France, put all the blame on the Germans, who had to pay $130 billion to the winners as compensation for the suffering they had caused. This was a ridiculously large sum that the German economy, destroyed by the war, could not pay. The German government printed more money and in 1926 the German economy collapsed so that almost everyone lost their money and people were very poor.

This was made worse by the GREAT DEPRESSION of 1929, which led to a collapse of jobs across the Western world. Everyone felt hopeless, people had no food and the future looked grim. Even in the US there were bread queues and there were no jobs to be had. People were desperate and these events helped lead to the rise of Hitler because he seemed to promise hope.

Hitler was elected as Reich President in 1932 and in January 1933 had himself declared State President and elections were done away with. He was tremendously popular and a marvelous speaker. He appealed to pride in being German and offered people a way forward. In particular he claimed that the problems of Germany were not the fault of the Germans but of Jews and Communists.

Blaming the Jews for all the problems of Germany made Hitler more popular. Jewish shops were looted and destroyed, synagogues were burnt to the ground and gangs of his supporters, the Black Shirts, went through the streets making people give the Hitler salute and destroying Jewish homes and shops. All Jews were made to wear the yellow star to show they were Jews and non-Jews were not allowed to do business with Jews.

The more wealthy Jews who could see what was happening tried to leave. Many went to the US and other countries (Albert Einstein was one Jew who was able to get out) However, many other Jews thought that, although times were hard, they would just do what they were told and things would somehow turn out all right. Also, Jews were not allowed to travel and many did not have much money and so could not travel. By the time many realized how serious things were, it was too late – they could not get out. Britain and other countries took some Jews in as refugees but many were also refused entry.

Ein feierlicher Augenblick von der Grundsteinlegung zum Haus der deutschen Kunst

Der päpstliche Nuntius Bajallo di Torregrossa spricht eben zum Führer:

„Ich habe Sie lange nicht verstanden.
Ich habe mich aber lange darum bemüht
Heute versteh' ich Sie."

Auch jeder deutsche Katholik versteht heute Adolf Hitler und stimmt am 12. November
mit:

„Ja"!

Hitler decided that Jews had to leave their homes and they were put into GHETTOS. Surrounded by barbed wire or walls, the ghettos were often sealed so that people were prevented from leaving or entering. Established mostly in Eastern Europe (eg Lodz, Warsaw, Vilna, Riga, Minsk but also in areas in Amsterdam), the ghettos were characterized by overcrowding, starvation and forced labour. These ghettos enabled the Germans to round up the Jews easily so that they could then be sent off to the death camps. Some tried to hide but dogs went in to sniff out those who did not leave and thousands were shot and bayoneted to death. This separation of the Jews into ghettos made it easier for Germans to regard them as "different", non-human and

unclean. They were seen as vermin that needed to be eradicated and the other German people did almost nothing to protest or help.

There was a special camp, Ebensee, kept by the Nazis to which young boys and girls were sent. These children were experimented on, in the so-called interests of medical science, by doctors who performed experimental operations on them (without any anaesthetics). They were the equivalent of today's rabbits, dogs, cats and mice that are used for experimentation. It was held that the benefits that would come from the experiments would more than outweigh any pain and, as the boys and girls were only Jews, they would be killed in any case.

Top: "Work makes you free" - the deceptive slogan over the entrance to one of the death camps. Middle: Cattle trucks used to transport Jews to the camps. Bottom: Railway lines leading to the death camps

When the Second World War broke out the Germans needed a huge amount of weapons and ammunition so many Jews were used as slave labour in factories. The conditions were terrible but at least those who worked in the factories were kept alive and had basic food. The film *Schindler's List* is the story of the bravery of one German factory owner who employed Jews and saved their lives – but few factory owners were like this. They used Jews as slaves to increase their profits. The Nazis were not mainly interested in the Jews as slaves – they wanted to get rid of them altogether. This led to what they called THE FINAL SOLUTION, which involved not simply putting the Jews into special camps but killing them. To do this, the Nazis built special camps in Eastern Europe and Jews were transferred from all over occupied Europe to these camps.

The Jews were transported to the camps by train but they were not in ordinary carriages. They were put into cattle trucks with no seats, no toilets and no food and they traveled for many days without being let out. Many died on the journey. Above the entrance gates of one of the largest camps, Auschwitz, were the words "Arbeit macht frei" "WORK MAKES YOU FREE". This was, of course, a lie. The only freedom for most of those who went into the camps was the freedom brought by death. Not only Jews went to these camps. Those who opposed the Nazis, those with physical disabilities, gypsies and homosexuals were also sent; the Nazis particularly despised homosexuals although the emphasis on "manliness" in some German army units made, some historians have claimed, homosexuality common.

The trains drew into the camps and the Jews were unloaded and put into dormitories. There was hardly any food and some tried to escape even though they knew that death was inevitable. In spite of this, in the camps, faith in God was maintained and the rabbis held services and tried to keep some hope alive.

Top: Jews wearing the yellow star
Bottom: Prisoners being helped by Russian guards at the end of the war

The guards were German or recruited from nations occupied by the Germans such as the Ukraine. The guards were vicious and uncaring but they were obeying orders and they believed that this meant they were doing what was right.

The Jews were stripped naked and men, woman and children were herded into concrete buildings, which they were told were showers. In fact these were gas chambers. After being locked in, gas was pumped in. The people inside screamed and shouted but after 40 minutes they were all dead. The hair was taken from the dead bodies to be used to stuff mattresses. Any gold teeth were knocked out and the gold melted down. Their bodies were then taken out and buried in mass graves.

Sometimes Jews were shot – they were lined up in front of mass graves so that, after they died, they would fall back into the pits in which they would be buried. But this was an expensive way of disposing of them. Gas was the preferred option.

When the allies reached the camps, they could not believe what they saw. They saw walking skeletons who could barely stand. The Germans had tried to conceal what had been done but they could not do so. The local Germans in the neighboring villages knew what was happening but did not ask questions and said it was nothing to do with them. Even the guards denied they had done anything wrong as they said they were obeying orders.

Sometimes human beings can find hope and God in the midst of the blackest despair. Elie Weisel, who himself survived the holocaust, tells the story of a group of rabbis who met in the camps and placed God on trial for his failure to protect his chosen people, Israel. Even though this could be seen as blasphemy – God could not be named and should be worshipped and obeyed – but Jewish rabbis have a long tradition of questioning and arguing with God. The trial duly commenced with arguments being put on both sides and eventually the verdict was reached – God was guilty and was condemned. The rabbis finished the trial and then went off to say Kiddush or night prayers. Even though the rabbis protested against God, and convicted God, they still worshipped and obeyed Him. This apparent contradiction lies at the heart of Jewish thought – God can be questioned but must always be obeyed and, in the greatest despair and evil, only God can provide hope and meaning.

LIGHT IN DARK PLACES

Two Young Jewish girls, one Dutch and one German – one 14 and one 27 – wrote diaries that bring to life the suffering and also the hope and faith that was found amidst the evil of the holocaust. The best known is Anne Frank, but the story of Etty Hillesum is, perhaps, more remarkable still.

ANNE FRANK

Anne Frank's father, Otto, was an officer in the German army in the First World War and he and his wife, Edith, were respectable, middle class German Jews. By 1933, Otto moved to Amsterdam as the family could see the effect of Hitler's policies. A year later, his wife and their two daughters, Margot and Anne (who was now four years old) joined Otto in Amsterdam. In May, 1940, Germany invaded Holland and the Frank family were once again living under Nazi rule. Anne Frank attended the local Montessori school, but after the summer holidays in 1941, she was not allowed to attend school with non-Jews.

By 1942 Jews were being arrested because they were Jews. Many were forced to go to German forced labour camps and the Frank family prepared to go into hiding in a small group of rooms above Otto Frank's offices. Friends and employees promised to keep the business running and also said that they would risk their lives to help the family survive. On July 5, 1942, Anne Frank's sister, Margot, received a call-up notice to be deported to a Nazi "work camp". On the evening of July 6, the family moved into their hiding place.

A week later, on July 13, another German Jewish family, the van Pels, joined the Franks. Eight people in total were in hiding and they stayed there for two years. The rooms were crowded and they had to be careful not to be seen or heard as if anyone knew they were there they would be arrested. They were finally betrayed, arrested and sent to prison and then to the Westerbrok transit camp. They stayed in this camp for a month before being put on a cattle truck train to the Auschwitz death camp in Poland. Tragically, it was the last Auschwitz-bound transport ever to leave Westerbrok.

In October 1944, Anne and Margot were taken from Auschwitz to the Bergen-Belsen concentration camp in Germany, which was a camp without food, heat, medicine or toilets. Thousands there died from planned starvation and epidemics. Anne and Margot, weak from living in the concentration camps, contracted typhus and died. Of the eight people who lived in the secret hiding place, only Otto Frank survived the war.

Anne Frank's diary survived the war, has been published and translated into 67 languages. It is a very moving story of the developments and hopes of a young girl who, instead of being at school and mixing with her friends, spent more than two years locked in small rooms waiting at any moment for the knock on the door which would signal that she and her family were to be taken off and killed. She knew what was happening by listening to the German radio – early in her diary she wrote on October 9, 1942:

"Our many Jewish friends and acquaintances are being taken away in droves. The Gestapo is treating them very roughly and transporting them in cattle cars to Westerbrok, the big camp in Drenthe to which they're sending all the Jews ... If it's that bad in Holland, what must it be like in those faraway and uncivilized places where the Germans are sending them? We assume that most of them are being murdered. The English radio says they're being gassed."

Two years later she was still hiding. Her youth was slipping away and the world seemed an evil place – yet Anne remained hopeful of the future and of the goodness of people. On July 15, 1944 she wrote:

"We're much too young to deal with these problems, but they keep thrusting themselves on us until, finally, we're forced to think up a solution, though most of the time our solutions crumble when faced with the facts. It's difficult in times like these: ideals, dreams and cherished hopes rise within us, only to be crushed by grim reality. It's a wonder I haven't abandoned all my ideals, they seem so absurd and impractical. Yet I cling to them because I still believe, in spite of everything, that people are truly good at heart.

"... And yet, when I look up at the sky, I somehow feel that everything will change for the better, that this cruelty too shall end, that peace and tranquility will return once more. In the meantime, I must hold on to my ideals. Perhaps the day will come when I'll be able to realize them!"

From Anne's diary, July 15, 1944

ETTY HILLESUM

Etty Hillesum, lived in Amsterdam and, like Anne Frank, ended up in the Westerbrok camp and was sent to her death on the cattle trucks. However whilst Anne Frank was a teenage girl living in hiding, Etty Hillesum was a fully-grown young woman who, although Jewish, was profoundly influenced by the Christian as well as the Jewish Scriptures. Etty's diary was begun in March 1941 when she was 27 years old and she continued writing it until she was sent to Auschwitz, where she died on November 30, 1943. The diaries written after October 13, 1942 were lost. There still remained, however, 1200 handwritten pages and 60 letters to various friends.

Etty was a complex young woman – she was proud to be Jewish but was not a practicing Jew. Instead of seeking to escape the terrors of Westerbrok, she voluntarily went to work there to help those who suffered and the people on their way to the death camps. She chose to work in hell and wanted to go on thinking and wrestling with God amidst the suffering. She said, "I would like to be the thinking heart of the whole concentration camp."

Etty was highly intelligent and, once the Nazis had invaded Holland, she well knew what was going to happen. Like all Jews, she had to wear the yellow star and she knew that all Jews were to be killed yet she wrote in her diary that 1941 was "a year that was for me the richest and most fruitful, and also the happiest of all". She said that life was beautiful and she loved life, but she refused to go into hiding even though this might have saved her life. Instead she went to work in Westerbrok and although, as a volunteer, she was allowed to come and go freely at first, when she was away from the camp she longed to return to the people there.

Etty read a great deal and St Augustine, Dostoyevsky and the Bible were her biggest influences. She came back more and more to the Bible – to the Psalms, which she found a continuous source of inspiration but also to many passages in the Christian Scriptures. One of her favourite passages was "Do not be anxious for tomorrow, for tomorrow will be anxious for itself" and she also loved 1 Corinthians 13. She wrote: *"The Bible is so rugged and tender, simple and wise."* In the middle of the most terrible evil, Etty found God. She wrote in July 1942: *"I am with the hungry, the tortured, the dying every day, but I am also near the jasmine and the piece of heaven outside my window. In life there is space for everything. For a faith in God and for a miserable death."*

She was convinced of the love and goodness of God in the middle of the most terrible evil, suffering and inhumanity. Etty was also convinced that God needed help – this seems, to some, a strange notion. Is God not meant to be all powerful? To Etty, however, it was not strange and she saw her life as aiding God in a constant struggle against evil and she saw herself as aided by the love of God and the beauty of the world, which was a mark of God's presence in it:

"I shall try to help You, God, to stop my strength ebbing away, though I cannot vouch for it in advance. But one thing is becoming increasingly clear to me: that you cannot help us, that we must help You to help ourselves. And that is all we can manage these days and also all that really matters; that we safeguard that little piece of you, God, in ourselves. And perhaps in others as well ... I bring you not only my tears and my forebodings on this stormy, grey Sunday morning, I even bring you scented jasmine. And I shall bring You all the flowers I shall meet on my way, and truly there are many of those. I shall try to make You at home always. Even if I should be locked up in a narrow cell and a cloud should drift past my small barred window, then I shall bring you that cloud, oh God, while there is still the strength in me to do so."

In the end, Etty was no longer a volunteer – she became like those she had tried so hard to help – an inmate. Still she sought to bring love and joy to people without thinking of herself at all. She tried to keep alive a spirit which saw beauty and goodness in a world full of evil and pain. When she was on the cattle truck, she managed to throw a postcard out of the truck and it was picked up by some farmers and posted. It said *"I open the Bible at random and I find this: "The Lord is my refuge". I am sitting on my rucksack in a crowded freight car ... the departure came rather unexpectedly, in spite of everything. A surprise order sent purposely for us from the Hague. We left the camp singing ..."*

It is hard to imagine the situation. Thousands of young and old Jews, many ill, herded under the guns of the guards into cattle trucks with no windows to go on a journey across Europe to the death camps – and yet they went from Westerbrok singing! However severe the reality and nature of evil, it cannot quench the power of love or the appreciation of beauty. Etty's journey to faith in God was a long and hard one – for a long time she could not find it in herself to use the word "God" at all. Etty found God inside her but she believed passionately that God lay within the hearts of all people and she saw it as her task to bring this out. When she looked at the faces of the cruel guards she wrestled with the enormous difficulty of the claim that human beings are created in the image of God – yet she knew this to be true, however hard it was to accept in the horror that was Westerbrok:

"If I think of the faces of the armed escort in green uniforms, my God, what faces! I observed them one by one, from my hidden position behind a window. I was never more frightened than by those faces. I had difficulty with the Word that is the leitmotif of my life: 'And God created man in his image'. This Word lived a difficult morning with me."

Etty thought deeply about evil but did not have the time to work out any clear answers. She wrote:

"Living and dying, sorrow and joy, the blisters on my exhausted feet and the jasmine behind the house, the persecution, the unspeakable horrors – it is all as one in me and I accept it all as one mighty whole and begin to grasp it better if only for myself, without being able to explain to anyone else how it all hangs together. I wish I could live for a long time so that one day I may know how to explain it, and if I am not granted that wish, well, then somebody else will perhaps do it, carry on from where my life has been cut short. And that is why I must try to live a good and faithful life to my last breath: so that those who come after me do not have to start all over again, need not face the same difficulties."

WHAT CAUSED THE HOLOCAUST?

The easy answer to the question is "Hitler" or, possibly, "Hitler and the Nazis". The easy answer is to say, "Those people were evil. They were responsible".

After the war, the allies wanted to put Nazi leaders on trial. Some escaped and some, including Hitler, committed suicide in the last days of the war. The NUREMBURG WAR TRIALS were held to put those who were caught on trial. The picture shows the trial with US guards lined up behind the prisoners and their lawyers. Most of those put on trial admitted what they had done but they claimed that they were innocent. They said that there was nothing wrong or evil in what they had done. Germany had a democratically elected government and had the right to rule itself however it chose. Whilst some unpleasant things had been done, they individually were just obeying orders.

This defence was not accepted and many of the Nazi leaders were condemned to death or put in prison for long periods for crimes against humanity. What is clear is that without these men the holocaust could not have happened. But they alone did not cause it.

If an attempt is made to explain how the holocaust happened and what the causes were, the following might be listed as contributory causes:

Top: Jewish children prisoners
Bottom: The Nuremburg trials

1. *The Treaty of Versailles had contributed to the rise of the Nazis. In recognition of this the allies launched a bold and imaginative plan to rebuild Germany after the Second World War, and did not seek to punish Germany but instead helped it to grow strong again and to become a democratic, independent country.*

2. *Hatred of the Jews had been common in Europe for nearly 2000 years. Passages in the Christian Gospels clearly blame the Jews for the death of Jesus. For instance Matthew's Gospel records Pilate wanting to release Jesus but the Jews insisting on him being put to death. Pilate says Jesus is innocent but the crowd insists and "the whole (Jewish) people said in reply, 'His blood be upon us and upon our children'." Christian popes, bishops, priests and ordinary people blamed the Jews and, indeed, the wearing of the yellow Star of David was not an invention of the Nazis but was insisted on by Christian leaders in Germany in the 13th century.*

3. *The Jews did not fully integrate but maintained their own identity (this was how they survived) with their own diet, dress, customs and language. This created suspicion and made them an obvious target when a scapegoat was needed.*

4. Many Jews were incredibly talented in art, science, music and business and this meant that many ordinary Germans were jealous of their success. When Hitler blamed "international financiers" (meaning Jews) for the plight of the German people many were happy to let them be blamed.

5. Hitler's own psychology and his background played a considerable part. He was a powerful and charismatic speaker, so it was not difficult for him to get a following. He had been a corporal in the German army in the First World War, and had been a lonely child.

6. Hitler appealed to pride in the German nation, he promised to restore German glory and nationalism was a popular message.

7. Hitler drew his support from those who had been most affected by the severe times Germany had been through. German social institutions had been destroyed, so even traditional German leaders could not resist him.

8. Once Hitler was in power, the opposition was too frightened to stand against him because they felt that their lives would be at risk. On January 30, 1933, he set up a dictatorship. In 1934, the chancelorship and presidency were united in the person of the Führer. Soon, all other parties were outlawed and opposition was brutally suppressed. Few were willing to stand against this exercise in power.

9. Neither the Catholic Church nor the main Lutheran Church condemned Hitler. In fact the

Catholic Church saw Hitler as a defender of Christianity against the threat posed by communism.

10. *Army personnel, guards and civilian officials were willing to obey orders. If they had not done so their lives would have been threatened. Throughout the countries occupied by the Germans, local people collaborated in betraying the Jews and helping to send them to the camps (although there were, of course, also some brave people who took part in the resistance to the occupying forces).*

11. *Ordinary people, religious people, professional people, in fact most people did nothing. Nobody stood against the Final Solution. Some went along with plans for the Final Solution even though they were uncomfortable about it, but most ordinary people, who knew that Jews were disappearing, did nothing.*

12. *Darwin's theory of evolution suggested that the way of the world was the survival of the fittest. This meant that the destruction of the weak was only helping nature along.*

The picture left is of the inside of a gas chamber – gas nozzles were designed to look like showers so that people would go in willingly. Another picture beneath is a grinder for human bones. It was used to destroy the bones of those who had been gassed after their bodies had been burnt. The aim was to destroy all evidence that the holocaust has happened.

The gas chambers, the bone grinder and much other equipment could only have been used and produced if many others than the Nazi's played their part. Companies designed and manufactured special shower heads and machines specifically to grind human bones and, to an extent, those who worked on the production lines share part of the responsibility for the use to which the machine was eventually to be put.

QUESTIONS FOR CONSIDERATION

1) What in your view, were the main causes of the holocaust?

2) Were Nazi guards who obeyed orders in death camps evil?

3) Which groups in your society are marginalised like the Jews in Germany?

4) If you had been in Germany in 1934, what would you have done?

CHAPTER NINE

ATHEISM AND PROTEST ATHEISM

Progress in the 20th century ran at an incredible pace. Change is part of life and if a person is not willing to engage with change – in the work place or in the home – they are likely to feel left behind, or that they soon will be! Progress in science has been colossal but this is the first time in history that questions of "science" and questions about ultimate meaning in life have become entirely separated. It is possible to study the human genome without considering what it is to be human, to understand all there is to know about the biology of the human body without thought about what makes a person. It is possible to live life at such a fast pace that there are no times for silence and reflection. This is perhaps the first time in history that it is possible to avoid serious consideration about the mystical and spiritual side of being human, and perhaps also the first time in history that a majority of people in some civilizations have rejected God without thought. This is not, however, the first time in history that people have rejected belief in God. There is a long history of those who have rejected the existence of God – some of these have done so because of the existence of suffering and evil in the world – philosophically evil is one of the most serious challenges to the existence of God. People who reject belief in God are called ATHE-ISTS.

There are three main types of atheists:

PRACTICAL ATHEISTS – these people live their lives as if there is no God. They are not philosophers, they do not look at arguments for and against

God's existence and come to the conclusion that there is no God – instead they just live as if God does not exist and ignore the question.

SPECULATIVE ATHEISTS – these are people who have thought deeply about the issue and have come to the conclusion that there is no God.

PROTEST ATHEISTS – these people believe that whilst there may be a God to trust in him is a mistake.

Three of the best known speculative atheists are David Hume, Bertrand Russell and A J Ayer – all of whom were philosophers and all were certain that God did not exist and they produced philosophic arguments which sought to prove this. These can be summarized briefly as follows:

1. DAVID HUME had three main arguments against the existence of God:

David Hume

a. *Firstly he claimed that religious faith tends to be based on miracles. These he defined as breaches in the laws of nature believed to have been brought about by the power of God, or some other invisible agent. He rejected all reports of miracles. We have, Hume claimed, constant experience that natural laws operate regularly and if we hear of someone walking on water or rising from the dead it is more likely that the reports have been exaggerated or made up than that they are true. It is far more likely, Hume held, that natural laws have held and that the reports of breaches of natural law were fabricated. If miracles, defined as above, provide no evidence for belief in God then it is more likely that God does not exist.*

b. *The apparent design of the world is another argument for the existence of God. Whilst Hume accepted that the universe COULD have been designed, he also thought that it was just as likely that it arose by chance and if this was the case then there is no need for God to have created or designed the world.*

c. Thirdly he argued that if God was really wholly good and all powerful then evil would not exist. However, evil clearly does exist so an all good and all powerful God cannot exist. Again, therefore, he held that the evidence points away from the existence of God.

REPLIES TO HUME INCLUDE: (a) The reports of many who record miracles are not to be dismissed as quickly as Hume claims. Many people who have experienced miracles are intelligent, well balanced people whose evidence should be taken seriously. It is also known that natural laws are not as fixed as they were assumed to be in Hume's day – they are no more than generalizations of the way the world normally works. Religious experiences, which are claimed by a very substantial number of people, can also be used to support religious claims and these are ignored by Hume.

(b) The sheer improbability of the precise conditions necessary for stars and planets to form – let alone life – is so unlikely that it is much more plausible that an intelligence was responsible for the universe than that it was simply a matter of chance (see "The Design Argument" in *The Thinkers Guide to God*). (c) A number of thoughtful and sophisticated arguments have been given (dealt with in *The Thinkers Guide to God)* as to why a good, all powerful God would allow evil to occur and Hume takes no account of these and does not even acknowledge them.

A J Ayer

2. A J AYER was a verificationist. This means that he argued that all statements were meaningless unless:

a. They could be verified by sense experience or, at least, one could say what would verify them, OR

b. They were tautologies – this means that they just define the meaning of a word. For instance "Spinsters are female" or "Squares have four sides" are tautologies. These may be true but they do not tell us anything about the spinster or square that we did not already know.

If, therefore, someone claimed "There are yellow bugs living below the surface of Mars" then Ayer would consider this statement to be meaningful as it would be possible to state what would verify this statement as being true – namely if an expedition went to Mars and found that there were yellow bugs living under the surface. However statements about God are meaningless because, according to Ayer, there is nothing that will verify them, no evidence that will show the statement that God exists is either true or false. The statement "God exists" has, therefore, no content at all – it is not saying anything. It is rather as if someone said "Boojums exist" and someone replied, "What is a Boojum? What is your evidence that there are Boojums?" to which the reply was given "Boojums are indefinable and there is no evidence that can be given for or against their existence. You cannot see them, but they do exist. Honest."

Ayer says that the statement "God exists" is rather like "Boojums exist" – it has no content, can be neither proved nor disproved and is therefore meaningless.

REPLIES TO AYER INCLUDE: The verification principle cannot be verified by its own criteria. The statement "A statement is meaningless unless it can be empirically verified'" is itself not able to be verified so is meaningless! What is more, acceptance of the verification principle means accepting that poetry, statements about the emotions, love, hope, pain etc which cannot be verified are meaningless – which, of course, they are not. Ayer thought that language worked on scientific principles and it is far more sophisticated than this. Wittgenstein showed that the meaning of language depends not on verification but on the way language is used by human beings and Ayer does not recognize this.

---

3. BERTRAND RUSSELL argued that God cannot exist because the claim that God is good is incoherent. He argues that God is good can be taken in two ways:

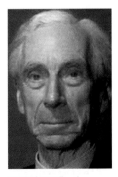

a. To say "God is good" means that there is a source of goodness independent of God against which God can be measured and held to be good – but in this case God is no longer supreme as there is a standard of goodness independent of God and so God is no longer the supreme creator of the universe as God is being judged against an independent standard which God did not create,

Bertrand Russell

OR

b. *To say "God is good" means that whatever God wants is good just because God wants it. In this case the statement that "God is good" just means that whatever God wants is good based on God's desires – God is the supreme autocrat, the supreme power figure. Russell argued this because, if there is no standard against which God can be judged good (as (a) above claims), then everyone has to accept God's definition of good. Russell pointed out that in the Hebrew Scriptures God is portrayed as commanding the death of women and children and the killing of thousands of people and the Israelites did this merely because God told them to. If this view is accepted, then God is not worthy of worship.*

Whichever alternative is taken, Russell argues, shows that the God of Christianity, Islam and Judaism either does not exist or is not worthy of worship because he is not good.

Replies to Russell include: Russell fails to recognize that good can be used in a variety of ways – he is guilty of assuming there is only one meaning of good – ie a moral meaning. However the Aristotelian tradition of philosophy and the Catholic Christian tradition that followed it has always claimed that something is good if it fulfils its nature. A good seagull or a good wombat fulfils the nature of a seagull or a wombat. Similarly a good human being fulfils the nature of what it is to be fully human. Once this is accepted, then Russell's challenge is irrelevant – God is not worshipped because God is morally good but because God is the source of the whole of the created order and, more important, because humans are intended for fellowship with God and this is the only end that will ultimately satisfy human beings. All other ends will result in disappointment and despair.

The above examples of speculative atheism demonstrate that a rejection of God has traditionally been rationally argued with great seriousness, not just asserted as opinion.

In Chapter Seven the implications of a denial of God leading to post-modernism were made clear. The consequence of a post-modern approach to good and evil is that human opinion becomes the final arbiter of good and evil. Evil can then be seen as relative and as something that will alter according to perspective. Then, it is possible, for example, to decide that the wholesale genocide of a race of people is necessary for what are considered to be good political ends. This becomes a valid choice based on the opinion of the day. If the modern world is to avoid this, grounds need to be found for asserting an absolute difference between good and evil. One way to do this is to maintain the existence of God. This is not without problems (For further discussion see *The Thinkers Guide to God*) and Protest Atheists significantly add to the difficulty. They have another challenge to offer based not on argument, but on the existence of innocent suffering.

PROTEST ATHEISM

Protest atheists believe in God. This seems a contradiction because surely the very definition of an atheist is one who does NOT believe in God?

The answer to this is "Yes", but protest atheists believe that God exists – but they reject God. They consider that whilst there is indeed a God who created and sustains the universe, this God should be cast off and condemned rather than worshipped. Their reason for holding this is generally the suffering caused by the existence of so much evil in the world. Protest atheists, therefore, accept God's existence but protest against God – they therefore reject God and refuse to worship or obey God. They are called "atheists" because of this (ie because of their rejection of God) not because they do not believe in the existence of God.

The origin of protest atheism lies in the most challenging attack ever mounted against the God of Christianity, Islam and Judaism. It was put forward in a work of fiction, a novel by the Russian writer, Dostoyevsky.

IVAN KARAMAZOV'S CHALLENGE

The novel *The Brothers Karamazov* features three sons of the old man Karamazov and they are very different. The three are Dimitri, Ivan and Alyosha. The key debate takes place between the middle brother, Ivan, and the younger brother, Alysoha. Ivan is something of a philosopher – he has left the family home and gone away to the big city where he has studied philosophy. He comes home after an absence of some years and gets acquainted with his younger brother, Alyosha, over dinner. They talk as would be expected after not seeing each other for some time and Ivan asks Alyosha whether he believes in God. Alyosha says that he does; more than that he has decided to become a novice monk and to join the local monastery where there is a very good and holy man called Father Zossima.

Ivan says that he, also, believes in the God who created the heaven and earth – he says:

"I accept God directly and simply" and *"I also accept His supreme wisdom and His purpose. I believe in the order and the meaning of life ... I believe in eternal harmony."*

However Ivan refuses to accept this world created by God. Ivan accepts that one day eternal harmony will be established but even then he will not accept God's world. He therefore rebels against God and refuses to accept God's authority. His grounds for doing this are the suffering of young children. Ivan cannot understand why young children have to suffer. A few pages earlier in the novel he has asked why a baby was crying. This is not a question as to the immediate causes – for instance whether the baby was hungry or had a wet nappy. Ivan's question is at a deeper level: Why do babies and young children cry? Why do they have to suffer?

Ivan gives three examples, which we now know were taken from Russian newspapers at the time:

1. *Turkish soldiers had invaded Bulgaria and because they were scared of an uprising by Russian Slavs, they treated the Slavs terribly. Ivan says: "Imagine: a mother stands trembling with an infant in her arms, around her the Turks who have entered. They fondle the infant, laugh in order to amuse it. They succeed, the infant laughs, At that moment a Turk points a gun at it, four inches from its face. The boy baby laughs joyfully, stretches out his little hands to grab the pistol and suddenly the soldier pull the trigger right in its face and smashes the little head to smithereens."*

2. *A little five-year-old Russian girl was constantly beaten, flogged and kicked by her parents. One night she did not ask to get up to go to the toilet and she wet her bed. The parents then locked her out all night "... in the outside cold and freezing latrine. What is more they smeared her eyes, cheeks and mouth all over with her faeces and compelled her to eat these faeces and it was the mother, her own mother, who did the compelling."*

> *3. There was a general who retired from the army and ran his great estate. He loved hunting and had many dogs and huntsmen and treated the people on his estate terribly. Then one day a young boy of eight threw a stone during a game and hurt the legs of the general's favourite hunting dog. He had the boy stripped and, in front of his mother, set him running off across the fields. He then set his hunting dogs on him and the boy was torn to pieces – in front of the mother.*

Ivan is saying to his brother Alyosha that NOTHING can justify the suffering of young children. He is not dealing with the suffering of adults, he accepts that they have "eaten the apple" (referring to the apple from the tree of the knowledge of good and evil taken from the garden of Eden), they know the difference between right and wrong. Perhaps, he is implying, they can be held to have brought any suffering they undergo on themselves – BUT THIS CANNOT BE THE CASE WITH YOUNG CHILDREN. They are innocent – and yet they suffer. Ivan says:

"Look. If everyone must suffer in order with their suffering to purchase eternal harmony, what have the children to do with it? It is quite impossible to understand why they should have to suffer ..."

Ivan is effectively saying that "the end cannot justify the means" – in other words he is claiming a principle that has long been accepted by traditional Christian writers that **it is never permissible to do or to allow evil so that good may come.** Take the following two examples:

• In the Third World, millions of people do not have proper drinking water and millions of children do not have enough to eat and cannot go to school. A relatively small amount of money will feed and educate a child for a year and this will give them a chance in life that they would not otherwise have. Would it be morally right to borrow an expensive item of jewellery, insure it and then lie about it being stolen or lost so that the insurance company pays out and then use the money to feed and educate, say, 10 African children for 10 years? Traditional Christian moral thinking would say "NO, THE END DOES NOT JUSTIFY THE MEANS".

• In Africa, millions are dying of AIDS because they cannot afford the drugs which would enable them to survive (in the western world these drugs are readily available and they enable people to live for a very long time indeed in spite of having AIDS but they are too expensive for those in poor countries). Assume that you have little money of your own and that you have been to Africa and know many people who are dying of AIDS. Would it be morally right to kidnap and torture a warehouse manager who has access to stocks of the drugs so that he will enable you to steal the drugs and give them to people you know in Africa who are dying? Traditional Christian moral thinking would say; "NO, THE END DOES NOT JUSTIFY THE MEANS".

Ivan Karamazov is saying exactly this – that no end can justify the means which he sees as the necessity of suffering. God, he claims, allows terrible evil and suffering to happen to innocent children AND WHATEVER END GOD HAS IN MIND, IT IS MORALLY WRONG FOR GOD TO ALLOW THIS EVIL TO TAKE PLACE. It is important to recognise that Ivan is accepting the traditional Christian, Islamic and Jewish view of God – namely that God is omnipotent and can do anything. He is effectively saying that God should be condemned because he allows evil to take place and nothing can justify this. Ivan is making a moral judgment on God based on what he accepts is his limited, human understanding and he knows that this is all that he has with which to work. He is effectively rejecting both the Augustinian and Irenean explanations about the source of evil. God is to blame for evil and the degree of innocent suffering in the world means that whatever plan God has in mind for humanity, it is not worth it.

Ivan is well aware that arguments can be put forward to justify God. Dostoyevsky would have known of the arguments of St Augustine and St Thomas Aquinas – he was well aware that philosophers and theologians can produce reasons why it would be right for God to allow evil. However he will not accept these arguments. He specifically rejects the arguments of "the bar room boys", as he puts it, who discuss the problem of evil over a few drinks. In the face of the suffering of innocent children, NOTHING, Ivan says, can justify God. This is why the second of the three examples above is so powerful as Ivan is saying that whatever the final end (even if the Lord, the parents and the child all embrace at the end of time and shout "Hosanna") NOTHING can justify the suffering. Ivan's examples are taken from Russian newspapers at the time but in the 20th and 21st centuries there are many more examples that can be given of innocent suffering:

- In 1943, in the Nazi death camps, they were running short of the gas used in the gas chambers. In some cases they took young children and threw them, alive, into the lime pits and then threw the dead bodies of adults on top of them. If young children tried to climb out, they were bayoneted to death by Ukrainian and other guards.

- In Rwanda, the majority tribe, the Hutus, killed 800 000 of their Tutsi neighbors within a month. They took machetes (long knives) and hacked the legs and arms off young children before throwing them, still alive in some cases, into the river in front of their parents. Children as young as nine or 10 were made to help and were given food for a bag of limbs, which they themselves had hacked off.

- In Vietnam, the United States dropped napalm (this is burning petroleum jelly which sticks to the skin and cannot be removed and burns fiercely until the person dies) on villages including children because they thought the villages harboured members of the Viet Cong who they were fighting.

- Under Pol Pot's regime in Cambodia, over one and a half million people were killed (including most teachers, civil servants and many who worked in towns) with children being killed just because their parents were middle class.

- In Bosnia, Serb soldiers systematically gang raped young girls as a deliberate war policy in order to impregnate the girls.

Alyosha, Ivan's brother and a novice monk, is appalled by Ivan's rejection of God and says "This is rebellion" and Ivan accepts that this is, indeed, the case. Ivan is rebelling against God. His rebellion is based on his humanity and his view that God should not have allowed little children to suffer no matter what God's purposes were. Ivan knows that God has all the power, he knows that he cannot change anything but he nevertheless refuses to accept God's power and rebels. This is where the term "protest atheism" comes from – it is a rebellion based on a protest against God.

Elie Weisel, who himself survived the holocaust, echos Ivan Karamazov in his book *The Night*:

"Never shall I forget that night, the first night in camp, which has turned my life into one long night, seven times cursed and seven times sealed. Never shall I forget that smoke. Never shall I forget the little faces of the children,

whose bodies turned into wreaths of smoke beneath a silent blue sky. Never shall I forget those flames which consumed my faith forever. Never shall I forget that nocturnal silence which deprived me, for all eternity, of the desire to live. Never shall I forget those moments which murdered my God and my soul and turned my dreams into dust. Never shall I forget these things, even if I am condemned to live as long as God Himself. Never."

Greenberg says that, following the Holocaust, *"Any statement, theological or otherwise, should not be made that would not be credible in the presence of burning children"*. In other words, unless theology (talk about God) can be done looking at the images of burning children, it is merely playing games. This is why the problem of evil is such a real challenge and why many have abandoned belief in God because of it.

Albert Camus

Camus said that his intention in writing his novel The Rebel was to help the reader understand the killing of 70 million people in the 20th century. Ivan Karamazov attacked God in the name of humanity and human beings then killed 70 million of their own.

Ivan places justice above God and the result, seemingly, is the holocaust. With the rebellion against God came the desire to maintain the divinity of man and the result has been a catastrophe.

It may, of course, be argued against Ivan that if God is going to create a world at all then evil has to be allowed. Ivan's response to this would be to say "Better no world than a world where children suffer". It is here, perhaps, that the weakness of Ivan's protest begins to emerge as whilst his position is at first persuasive, if the choice is really between no universe at all and a world where terrible evil and suffering does, indeed, take place but where there is also extraordinary beauty, compassion, self-sacrifice and love, then few people would easily say that it would be better if there was no world at all. Every parent who knowingly brings a child into the world is at fault by Ivan's criteria, because every child will suffer to some degree.

Whilst Ivan Karamazov's rebellion against God is the best-known example there is a much older example from the Hebrew Scriptures, which takes a very similar position to Ivan but arrives at a totally different conclusion.

JOB

The book of Job in the Hebrew Scriptures is quite extraordinary. It starts with God talking to Satan (who is NOT the devil but the prosecutor in God's court). God says: "Have you noticed my servant Job, and that there is no one on earth like him, blameless and upright, fearing God and avoiding evil?" Satan's reply is that this is not surprising – Job has everything. A lovely family, health and great wealth – of course he would be good. God effectively then makes a bet with Satan as he tells him that he can take away all his possessions and Job will stay faithful (William Blake has a series of paintings portraying the story of Job – the one below is of Job's family before their destruction). Satan wipes out all Job's family and destroys all his flocks and herds. He is left with nothing. Job cannot understand but he remains faithful to God and says:

"Naked I came forth from my mother's womb, and naked shall I go back again. The LORD gave and the LORD has taken away; blessed be the name of the LORD!"

William Blake. Job with his family before destruction

God effectively says to Job "Told you so!" but Satan (left Blake's painting Satan before the Throne of God) replies "Yes, but Job himself has not been touched. Let me hurt him and he will soon turn and curse you." God tells Satan he can do what he likes to Job – only he must not kill him. So Satan goes and covers him with severe boils from his feet to his head (William Blake's painting bottom right shows Satan pouring out the boils over Job who is lying down).

William Blake. Satan before the Throne of God

Job cannot understand what is happening to him – he trusts in God and believes himself to be innocent yet the suffering that has come upon him is immense. Even his wife, the only member of his family who is left says:

"Are you still holding to your innocence? Curse God and die."

Job, however, refuses to accept that his suffering is a punishment sent by God and he turns on his wife and says:

"Are even you going to speak as senseless women do? We accept good things from God; and should we not accept evil?"

Three friends of Job come to him (Eliphaz, Bildad and Zophar). They start by just sitting silently with him for seven days so great is their sorrow at the state he is in. Then they try to offer him comfort by suggesting explanations for his suffering. In fact, comfort is the very last thing they offer in doing this. They effectively say to Job that he must be being punished. The theology of the time is very clear – God rewards and protects those who are good and he punishes those who are guilty. Job is being punished so he must be guilty. He should confess before God and ask for forgiveness.

120

Job's reaction to this is a turning point in theology because:

- *He refuses to accept his friends' analysis.*

- *He refuses to accept that God works like this.*

- *He refuses to see his suffering as a punishment from God.*

Job remains faithful to God and does not accept that he has done anything wrong, at least nothing that would justify this suffering.

Gradually Job's anger against God increases:

"Know then that God has dealt unfairly with me, and compassed me round with his net.

If I cry out 'Injustice!' I am not heard. I cry for help, but there is no redress."

His initial anger is about his own suffering but it gradually develops until he is angry about innocent suffering in general. He knows that God is a God of

William Blake. Satan smiting Job with boils

power and that God is just, yet the innocent suffer. God seems to be unjust. The weak are trodden in the mud and the vice ridden and those who do wrong prosper:

"Why do the wicked survive, grow old, become mighty in power?...Their homes are safe and without fear, nor is the scourge of God upon them."

Job gets more and more angry with God, so much so that he wants to put God on trial. He knows that no one can see God and live and he asks whether God will destroy him for his impertinence but he is sure that this will not happen. Job is angry with God but believes God will listen to his anger – because it is just.

Next comes a young man, Elihu, who joins his argument to those of Job's three friends. However his argument is different from theirs. Elihu says that God has his reasons and Job is in the wrong to question God's ways. In a very significant verse, Elihu says:

"For he (Job) is adding rebellion to his sin by brushing off our arguments and addressing many words to God."

Just as:

1. Ivan is accused by his brother Alyosha of rebelling against God, so

2. Job is accused by Elihu of rebelling against God.

The key difference between the two is that Job's rebellion starts from a position of faith. Job rejects Elihu's position and continues to maintain his innocence and to challenge God. Finally in the last chapters of the Book of Job, God answers Job out of a whirlwind (see Blake's painting).

God is angry with Job's three "comforters", but not with Job and his answer entirely supports Job's position. Job is right to question, but how can Job hope to understand God:

"Where were you when I founded the earth? Tell me, if you have

William Blake. *The Lord answering Job out of the whirlwind*

understanding.

Who determined its size; do you know? Who stretched out the measuring line for it?...

Do you know about the birth of the mountain goats, watch for the birth pangs of the hinds ...

Who has given the wild ass his freedom, and who has loosed him from bonds?

I have made the wilderness his home and the salt flats his dwelling ...

Will the wild ox consent to serve you, and to pass the nights by your manger?....

Do you give the horse his strength, and endow his neck with splendour? ...

Is it by your discernment that the hawk soars, that he spreads his wings toward the south?
Does the eagle fly up at your command to build his nest aloft? ..."

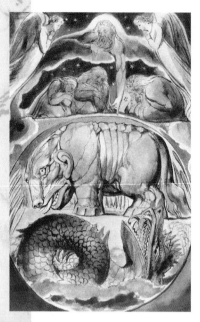

William Blake. Behemouth and Leviathan

(These are extracts from a long speech by God covering chapters 39 to 40 of the Book of Job.)

God is effectively saying that Job is right to challenge God about the problem of evil, right to reject the simplistic solutions of his friends but, in the end, Job is only a human being and cannot possibly begin to understand the complex and mysterious ways of God. Job is called upon to accept his role as creature before his creator. He has to trust God even though he cannot understand. Job, accepts this and this is, perhaps, the only possible response to Ivan Karamazov. In the final section of the book of Job, God says that even Leviathan and Behemoth (the forces of chaos – shown in Blake's painting as an elephant and a sea-serpent) are under God's control.

Perhaps philosophy comes to an end in the confrontation between Ivan Karamazov and Job:

- *Standing by the waters of the rivers of Rwanda, watching the bodies of the children float past with their arms and legs hacked off,*

- *Looking at the tens of thousands of dead in Cambodia or in Stalin's death camps*

- *Seeing the crying man who was abused and beaten constantly when he was a seven-year-old boy by older boys at his boarding school,*

- *Watching the weeping 12-year-old girl gang raped by 26 Serb soldiers,*

In these situations, philosophical arguments are of no importance and two human reactions are possible:

1. Ivan Karamazov stands in judgment on the God who would allow this suffering. God appears to him to be volatile and unjust in His dealings with humans. God might exist, but he is certainly not worthy of worship. Ivan rebels against God and rejects God effectively saying, "better no world at all than this world where innocent children suffer. I reject you God and I will not worship you or obey you."

2. Job stands next to Ivan and his starting point is the same. He might say, "Ivan I agree with you about your anger, I agree with you about the injustice of this, I shout and rage against the God who allows these terrible things to happen but, in the final analysis, I trust God even though I cannot understand Him. I cannot see how the suffering of children can possibly be worth it, but even though I cannot see it I believe that in some way it is. I can do no more."

During the Holocaust, in the face of the most terrible suffering of innocent people, those such as Anne Frank, Etti Hellisum and others did not feel that God was absent. In fact Etti Hellisum found God in those who suffered as much as in those who caused the suffering, as much as in the scented jasmine. Many others sustained belief in God. **What is certainly true is that, after the holocaust, philosophy and theology must be done in the presence of the worst forms of evil and suffering if these are to be taken seriously. They are not simply academic games - they affect the lives of all human beings too deeply. At the end of the day the problem of evil is not simply an intellectual problem - it is a challenge that confronts all of us and which demands a response.**

QUESTIONS FOR CONSIDERATION

1. What is the difference between a practical atheist, a speculative atheist and a protest atheist?

2. Which of the atheistic arguments against the existence of God in this chapter do you find most convincing and why?

3. Do you agree with Ivan Karamazov that NOTHING can justify the suffering of innocent children? Would you also agree with him that it would be better to have no universe at all than a universe that included the suffering of children?

4. Why did Job's reaction to his comforters represent a turning point in theology?

5. Is rational argument of any use when confronting horrendous evil? If not, then should one rely simply on emotion and, if so, how does one tell whether one's emotional reaction is right or not?

CHAPTER TEN

EVIL AND THE HUMAN PSYCHE

Various approaches have so far been examined which have seen evil as real and as existing independently of the human psyche. There has been a whole range of alternatives including:

1. *Cosmic dualism, which considers there are two fundamental forces in the universe – one good and one bad.*

2. *The view that there is a single force which gives rise to two subsidiary forces and these two subsidiary forces are good and evil.*

3. *The view that it is the material world that is evil and that renunciation of all desire and of anything that has to do with matter is the only way to overcome evil.*

4. *Belief in a single, all-powerful God who creates and uses evil to bring about God's purposes.*

5. *Belief in a single, all-powerful God whose will gives freewill and as a result evil comes into the world.*

However all these views were challenged by modern psychology which, in most of its forms, sees no need to consider God or the devil or any absolute power of good or evil. Evil is seen as a metaphysical term which is outside psychology's concern although psychology would see behaviour that is labelled as "evil" as something that can be explained by psychological factors and that can be changed and "cured" by the application of psychological techniques. Psychology, therefore, places the human being firmly at the center and renders talk of a force of evil irrelevant and unnecessary – except, of course, for the immensely strong force of evil in the human psyche which can cause such terrible damage and suffering.

Sigmund Freud was one of the first and possibly the greatest of the early psychologists. Freud's influence has been immense although many modern day psychologists dismiss his work as unscientific. As an atheist and with no interest or belief in the spiritual side of human life he saw evil as having no independent existence. He located it entirely in the human psyche. He was influenced by Nietzsche who denied that there was any God and claimed that good and evil should be decided by the individual (see Chapter 7). In many ways Freud provided a natural working out of the idea that "God is dead". His approach seems to many psychologists to be based on theories that cannot be proved. In spite of this, Freud is of great importance particularly in drawing attention to the power of the unconscious mind and of the importance of sexual development.

Many modern psychologists follow Freud in rejecting God but nevertheless some consider that religion and belief in God is a powerful tool in helping people to come to terms with the complexity of their psyche. Others consider that psychology alone is needed to explain human behaviour. Some so-called

Freud

Freud saw himself as a scientist following a scientific method. He considered that there were three great moments in history that had redefined what it was to be human:

1. Through Copernicus' discovery that the sun went round the earth, human beings lost their place at the center of the Universe

2. Through Darwin's theory of evolution, human beings ceased to be seen as distinct from animals.

3. Through Freud, human beings came to see that they were not even in control of their own minds or their actions.

A legitimate challenge is to consider whether science can understand the complexity of what it is to be human. Some would say there is something "more" that science does not grasp.

"**behaviourists**" consider that human beings can be defined entirely in terms of their actions and behaviour and this behaviour can be conditioned by suitable training rather like Pavlov's dogs. (Pavlov gave his dogs a routine so that whenever the dogs were fed, a bell was rung. The dogs learned to associate the bell with food. The result was that the bell alone would make them produce saliva whether or not there was any food.) Behaviourists attach little importance to the inner workings of the mind and reject any spiritual dimension – whether good or evil – of human beings. Social conditioning is central to behaviourists and human beings are seen, at least to some degree, as clay that can be manipulated by creating the right social and psychological conditions for human development. In taking this approach, however, they have moved a long way from Freud and Jung, and so it is to these founders that attention needs to be initially directed in understanding the approach to evil take by psychology.

Libido

Freud recognized that a dangerous situation could arise when people identify themselves as a member of a group or society. He suggested that libido attachment to a single object can take place on a mass scale. This effectively produces a society in which everyone has "fallen in love" with one object. This he suggests is what happened in Germany in the 1930s when the German people identified with each other through their common "love" for Hitler. Books by Freud were burnt by the Nazis in 1933 and Freud commented that this showed progress as in the middle ages he would have been burnt. In fact Freud was wrong – the Nazis would have gassed him first, as they did his sisters because he was of Jewish ancestry.

SIGMUND FREUD

Freud (1856-1939) was born in what is now called the Czech Republic, but was then the Austro-Hungarian Empire. Freud was a convinced atheist who was committed to persuading others to his view although he was interested in the role religion played in people's minds. In one essay, "A seventeenth century demonological neurosis", Freud analyzed the paintings and writings of Christopher Haizman, a 17th-century painter who considered that he had a pact with the devil. Haizman believed he had a pact with the devil but Freud calls this a neurosis, which means that he believed that the so-called "pact" could be explained by psychological factors. Freud did not look outside of the human mind for the devil or any force of evil. Evil instead was something that Freud explained in terms of the sub-conscious mind. This picture by Leonardo da Vinci of "Madonna and child with St Anne" was in Freud's study. In the painting Mary is seated on St Anne's knee. St Anne is watching over the shoulder of Mary, hand on hip at if keeping an eye on what Mary is doing. This, for Freud, is how the subconscious mind works – the conscious mind (the ego) thinks that it is in control and is acting freely, but in fact it is completely restrained by the sub conscious (the super-ego). In this painting Mary is free to play with her son, but is not free to do so without the watchful eye of the subconscious mind, represented by St Anne. These two illustrations perhaps give a brief insight into Freud's theories about evil and its place in the human mind.

Freud's analysis of the human psyche was heavily influenced by what he saw as human sexual development particularly in the early stages of infancy and in childhood. In this growing process, which is shared by all human beings, the Oedipus complex is central. According to Freud the Oedipus complex emerges between the ages of three and five. A male child will see the father as competing with him for the mother's love. A female child will compete with the mother for the father's love. If a person fails to progress adequately through this stage they can become fixated. This means that they remain attached to objects associated with this stage, for example a person fixated in the Oedipal stage may choose sexual partners who resemble their parents. In attempting to master this complex revolving round love and jealousy directed towards the parents, most psychological problems arise and these are deeply imbedded in the growing child's super-ego, or subconscious mind. Freud tried to explain religion in

Parts of the mind

For Freud, the mind consists of three parts:

an ego which contains a person's ordinary thoughts and directs daily behaviour, This is "reality orientated" as it focuses on the everyday world.

an id containing all the instincts and repressed feelings and

a superego which maintains the person's values and prohibitions and controls the ego through guilt. Trauma in childhood can upset the balance between the three and the ego can become the site of intrapsychic conflict between an intruding id and a threatening superego. The result can be neurosis, depression and anxiety.

Leonardo da Vinci. Madonna and child with St Anne

Freud's psychosexual stages of development

ORAL STAGE – *from birth to one and a half years.* **Erogenous Zone in Focus:** *Mouth.* **Gratifying Activities:** The mother's breast is the only source of food and nourishment and the mouth is central as the baby sucks, bites and swallows. If the child gets stuck in this stage then symptoms later in life will include smoking, chewing on pens, pencils, etc, nail biting, overeating and sarcasm (represented by the "biting personality").

ANAL STAGE – *from one and a half to three years.* **Erogenous Zone in Focus:** *Anus* **Gratifying Activities:** Going to the toilet and the power that comes from not going. Toilet training is vital as the child learns that it has the power to please or anger the parents and for the first time has power over them. If the child does not develop through this stage, maybe because the parents are over-anxious or they fail to train the child, then it will become either very disorganised, reckless, defiant and careless or it will be obsessively clean, obstinate and seek to conform or show passive aggression.

PHALLIC STAGE – *aged four to five.* **Erogenous Zone in Focus:** *Genitalia.* **Gratifying Activities:** playing with his or her genitalia. The key feature of this stage is that the child, according to Freud, becomes aware of its identity as a sexual being and is attracted to the parent of the opposite sex. The child also feels envy or fear of the same sex parent. In boys this is the "Oedipus complex" by which the boy is meant to be sexually attracted to his mother (named after the man in a Greek myth who killed his father and married his mother), whilst for girls it is the "Electra complex". Boys in the oedipal stage are said by Freud to fear being castrated by their fathers because of their love for their mothers whilst girls discover that they have already been castrated. They may feel hostile towards their mother for bringing them into the world "in this shape". They may envy men, as they do not have a penis. When the girl then discovers that she is the same shape as her mother her relations with her father may feel more free. Freud considers that the child needs to resolve its feelings of conflict and move on to the next stage, but if it cannot then it will have permanent feelings of envy and hostility. Freud seemed to consider that women never pass fully beyond the stage of wishing that they had a penis. At the end of this stage the Oedipus complex is repressed.

LATENCY STAGE – *age from five up to puberty.* **No erogenous zone.** During this period Freud considered that sexual feelings are suppressed and children focus on other aspects of life. Ideas and impulses associated with the oral, anal and phallic stages are pushed into the unconscious and denied expression. BUT the sexually organised memories of the three stages will influence the future. During this period, same sex friendships and social inter-action outside the home are developed.

GENITAL STAGE – *from puberty onwards.* Masturbation and heterosexual relationships become the focus. With the development of genitalia, children's sexuality is re-awakened. Freud considered that maturity here is only possible if the previous stages have been navigated successfully. If, therefore, there are problems at this stage then these will be due to problems at an earlier stage. As an example, if during the Oedipal stage the individual has not managed to come to terms with relationships with his or her parents, he or she may not be able to form adult relationships.

these terms, as an attempt by individuals to come to terms with the Oedipus complex. For Freud, the key to understanding human behaviour lies in the sexual development of human beings. Sexual feelings are repressed and this lies at the heart of difficulties in the unconscious mind. He analyzed a number of stages of human development:

It is possible, according to Freud to become stuck in one of these stages or to regress into it. The person will not understand their behaviour, but will act compulsively. Only a small part of what is in the mind is conscious, the rest is unconscious and made up of inadmissible and involuntary ideas which drive behaviour.

Freud relates not only individual development but also social systems to man's need to repress basic sexual and aggressive instincts. He traces the origins of human society back to a primal herding in which the sons had to fight the father for mating rights. He even speculates that **"during the human family's primeval period, castration used actually to be carried out by a jealous and cruel father upon growing boys"** (*Totem and Taboo*). This is one of the most bizarre of Freud's ideas and today would be considered laughable – but it indicates the extent to which Freud was willing to speculate with little or no evidence to support his speculation.

Freud attached great importance to myths and saw in them supportive evidence for his work. The myths provided insights into human psychology. Christianity he saw as being based on the myth of the sin of the first man, Adam, against God. Adam being in the wrong before God, Freud claimed, is the pre-cursor of each human who is in the wrong against his or her father. This wrong has to be placated and the God or father figure appeased.

St George slaying the dragon

Freud claimed that Christianity says that Jesus laid down his own life to appease the anger of the father but, he held, in all ancient religious traditions the idea was that a life only had to be given in exchange for a life. The original sin that needed appeasement was, Freud claimed, not simply disobedience before God (as Genesis records) but the murder of the father. This human wish for love from the father and yet the wish to murder the father lies at the heart of all religion. All human beings long for an unconditional, loving father figure who can accept them as they are and forgive all the dark sides of their character, so the religious idea of God is a projection of the human imagination and is the means whereby humans cope with the lack of love and the lack of meaning in the world. Christianity, says Freud, has at its heart the murder of the old Father and the substitution of the new son – it represents exactly what happens within the human psyche.

Freud considers that talk of evil is related to the evil actions performed by human beings and these are actions that stem from the unconscious mind and from a failure of development during the childhood process. Psychoanalysis can help people to come to terms with the difficulties in their pasts – especially conflicts relating to libido or sex-

"The Unconscious"

Freud created a new picture of the mind. Unreason, not reason, was at the centre.

Think of the mind like the sea. Humans are conscious of just the top layer but below this is the great, dark, unexplored depth of the unconscious – full of strange monsters (like the dragon in the picture). This led to the development of "depth psychology" in which the unconscious could be explored through psychoanalysis and some of these monsters identified. Freud hoped to found a science that would provide rational mastery over the unconscious.

ual desire and aggression ("thanatos") – and to move beyond the developmental stages into which they may have become locked.

One of the best ways of representing the dramatic shift of view that Freud represents is by reference to a painting of which he kept a copy in his private collection – this is the painting by Vittore Carpaccio of St George Slaying the Dragon. The painting has long been considered as an example of the forces of good (St George) slaying the force of evil (the devil represented by the dragon). However Freud would not have seen it like this – for Freud the dragon represents those dark forces of the unconscious mind that frequently drive human actions. These forces do, indeed, need to be combated and destroyed but the way to do this is not through the myths of religion but through science and, in particular, the science of psychoanalysis. This is a good example of a painting being interpreted by one generation in a way that a previous generation would not have recognised – but nevertheless finding real insight and relevance in the painting.

In the film *The Fisher King*, the "demons" within the central character (played by Robin Williams) are represented by a red knight on a red steed breathing fire and surrounded by fire – but the image is in his head although to him it is very real indeed. The red knight surfaces at key moments and takes control of him. He can see the knight coming and runs from it in terror but he cannot, of course, escape as what he runs from is within his own psyche.

Freud considered that the source of evil was the human mind, but that individuals could not always understand or control their behaviour. The solution was to be found in psychoanalysis, a process by which the person is made consciously aware of the influences of the unconscious mind.

Buddhism and Freud

There are extraordinary parallels between Freud's analysis of the unconscious and the Buddha's analysis of the human condition. According to Freud, the life wish (Eros which corresponds to the Buddhist idea of desire) and the death wish (very similar to the Buddhist principle of negativity, Mara) are the two drives which motivate individuals from within and dominate the day-to-day world. In both Buddhism and Freudian psychoanalysis the way to dispel these illusions is by an inner journey – either psychoanalysis or meditation.

The aims of the two systems are, however, different. Psychoanalysis aims to help people to live successfully within the world (the aim of psychoanalysis is for people to live and to work), whereas Buddhism seeks to extinguish desire and any sense of ego or self altogether in order to provide a root to seek release from the world in order to enter Nirvana.

CARL GUSTAV JUNG

Carl Gustav Young

Carl Gustav Jung was born in Switzerland in 1875. He studied medicine and, in 1907, he met Sigmund Freud in Vienna and the two men were soon working together. However Jung came to differ sharply from Freud and he developed analytical psychology (whereas Freud had developed psychoanalysis). For a start Jung did not consider that general theories could capture the complexity of individual human beings and he thought that the whole idea of the purpose of human beings had to be taken into account in working out the questions of meaning that were so important for understanding the human psyche. In short he felt that Freud had overstated the influence of childhood sexual development in the origins of mental disorders.

Jung considered that humans have a natural propensity to create myths that imbue their lives with meaning, but in the modern world it becomes more difficult for individuals to participate in the collective understanding that myths represent. Myths therefore tend to be discarded and the result is that meaning is discarded as well. It is through myth that the human sub-conscious becomes conscious and the emphasis on reason results in the unconscious remaining buried. The task of psychology is, therefore, to help individuals to integrate the different aspects of their psyche through the process of INDI-VIDUATION, which is effectively the same as self-realization. This individuation process requires each individual to come to knowledge of their sub-conscious – something that few do and, therefore, they tend to be at a shallow level of understanding about themselves.

THE COLLECTIVE UNCONSCIOUS

Although Jung's work concentrated on individuals he nevertheless considered that the unconscious minds of all human beings share something derived from the common past of humanity. Like Freud, Jung argued that the unconscious part of the mind contains personal drives and experiences of which the individual is not aware (see "The Shadow" on p.137). However, unlike Freud, Jung thought that members of every race share a deeper level of unconsciousness that he called the Collective Unconscious. Jung, in conversation with the South African novelist Laurence van der Post said: "that the more I looked into my own spirit and the spirit of my patients, I saw stretched out before me an infinite objective mystery within, as great and as wonderful as a sky full of stars spread out above us on a clear and moonless winter's night." If this is valid then deep within the unconscious mind are shared myths and ideas and these contain truths about the nature of the human condition that are passed on through countless generations. However there is no scientific evidence that these myths and ideas exist – which is one reason why Jung's work is largely discarded by many modern psychologists.

Human beings are, therefore, individuals but they also share their humanity with all other human beings and the marks of the past generations from whom they are descended are found in their subconscious minds.

For Jung, as for Freud, evil actions done by human beings can at least partly be explained by the operation of the unconscious mind and the task is to help the people who perform these acts to come to an understanding of what is happening within their own psyche. Jung himself was far more open than Freud to the positive side of religion and in his written work he was agnostic about whether or not there was a God or a power of evil. However, he considered that there are various archetypes buried deep in the human unconscious and one of these is the archetype of God. All that science could know was the role of the archetypes, but whether these represented an "imprint" of something beyond the human mind was, he considered, an unanswerable question – albeit one that Jung spent most of his life trying to resolve. **Having said this, Jung was asked on a BBC "Face to Face" interview if he believed in God. He said, "I do not believe ..." and then paused for quite a while and then added, "I know."**

As Jung makes clear in the passage on the next page about war, the origin of evil lies in human beings. However because most people always want to think positively about themselves they refuse to recognize this and therefore do not address it. People say they do not want war but according to Jung this is precisely what a part of them, a part that they fail to acknowledge, does want. They therefore do nothing to avoid war because they fail to recognize that war is precisely what they do want. He suggests that if humans made up a god of

Jung on the causes of war

" ... nobody wants war, but everybody goes to war ... we play with the idea of war, because it is a wonderful sensation. Yet we do not recognize this; therefore we are convinced that we don't want a war ... Now if a terrible god were influencing mankind, or a dangerous devil, we would ask ourselves what we could do to propitiate him and prevent such a catastrophe. But we think there is no such thing, no devil, no god, no ruling power. Who then makes a war?

Just as we don't want a war, we are also capable of wanting it only we don't know it ... we must admit that in no other time have there been so many people crowded together in Europe. It is a brand new experience. Not only are we crowded in our cities, we are crowded in other ways; we know practically everything that happens in the world, it is shouted on the radio, we get it in the newspapers ... we are impressed with all the misery of the world, because the whole world is now shouting in our ears every day. We enjoy it and we don't know what it is doing to us until finally we get the feeling that it is too much. How can one stop it? We must kill them all.

When I was in India I talked with certain people of Swaraj party who want Home Rule. I said: "But do you assume that you can run India with your party? - Do you not realize that in no time you would have a terrible quarrel between the Mohammedans and the Hindus? - they would cut each other's throats, they would kill each other by the hundreds of thousands." "Yes, naturally," he said, "they would." "But don't you think that is awful? – they are your own people." "Oh well, for those worthless chaps to cut each other's throats is alright, we have an increase in population of 34 millions these last ten years."

We think we are good and we are, yes, we have the best of intentions sure enough, but so you think that somewhere we are not nature, that we are different from nature? No, we are in nature and we think exactly like nature ... So we should say – and I would like to say – that there is a terrible demon in man that blindfolds him that prepares awful destruction, and it would be much better if we had a temple for the god of war ... we could say: "The god of war is restless, we must propitiate him, let us sacrifice to the god of war." And then every country would be going to the temples of the war god to sacrifice, perhaps it would be a human sacrifice, I don't know ... That would help. To say that it is not we who want it would help because man could then believe in his goodness. For if you have to admit that you are doing just what you say you are not doing, you are not only a liar, you are a devil, and then where is the self esteem of man? How can he hope for a better future? We can never become anything else because we are caught in that contradiction, on the one side we want to do good and on the other we are doing the worst.

How can man develop? He is forever caught in that dilemma. So you had better acknowledge the evil, what you call it doesn't matter. If there were priests who said that the god of war must be propitiated that would be a way of protecting yourself. But of course there are no such things, so we must admit that we prepare the war, that we are just thirsty for blood, everybody." (Excerpt from Jung's "Psychological-Analysis of Nietzsche's Zarathustra", a seminar given by Jung in Zurich 1938)

war, who would have to be placated by sacrifices, then at least they would be recognizing an inclination to go to war – even if not willing to see it in themselves – but the threat of war would be much reduced because everybody would be placating the god of war. At present we tend to think war is inevitable and not act.

The Shadow

The shadow is central to Jung's understanding of the human condition. There, he maintained, are two parts of every human being:

1. *The first is the ego and this is that part of every person of which they are conscious but there is another side,*

2. *The shadow, of which we are unaware.*

Every person is made up of these two parts but most people are only aware of their conscious selves and do not know of the unconscious side. Human beings are born as one person but during their lives two emerge – the ego and its shadow counterpart. Jung considered that from the teenage years on through the first part of life until about the mid forties humans concentrate on the ego and develop their careers, marry, acquire property and material possessions. These are all those things that the ego values and, in the meantime, the shadow side of every human being is ignored. This often leads to a mid-life crisis when a person has devoted themselves to the ego and the conscious side

Every human being has a shadow side

Jung's Dream

"I had a dream which both frightened and encouraged me. It was night in some unknown place, and I was making slow and painful headway against a mighty wind. Dense fog was flying along everywhere. I had my hands cupped round a tiny light which threatened to go out at any moment. Everything depended on my keeping this little light alive. Suddenly I had the feeling that something was coming up behind me. I looked back, and saw a gigantic black figure following me. But at the same moment I was conscious in spite of my terror, that I must keep my little light going through night and wind regardless of all dangers. When I awoke I realized at once that the figure was my own shadow on the swirling mists, brought into being by the little light I was carrying. I knew too that this little light was my consciousness, the only light I have. Though infinitely small and fragile in comparison with the powers of darkness, it is still a light, my only light."

For Jung, our shadow side is an integral part of what we are

of who they are and recognises that much of their life is empty and devoid of meaning. It is then that, if the person is self-aware, they may come to deal with the shadow side and finally, before they die, they may be able integrate the shadow and the ego to come back into a unity.

Every positive action has a shadow side and every person suppresses this side. This is one reason why people who are highly creative such as great painters and artists often have another side which may force itself to the surface if it is neglected, just as those who neglect their own creativity may find the urge to be creative coming out of the shadow and demanding attention.

Every human being is made up of a masculine and feminine side, yet often people will neglect one side of their personality and this then forms part of their shadow. A "man's man" may suppress his whole feminine side and therefore not be able to come to wholeness. Jung spent much time seeking to find ways to recapture the lost feminine principle in many male individuals and, indeed, in society as a whole. The same applies, of course, to women who too often neglect the male side of their personality. Again, many modern psychologists would reject Jung's position here, as they would see gender as being largely socially constructed rather than something that is innate.

In order to live in society everyone has to obey the structures of the society in which they live – otherwise human life would be impossible. But this means that people have to suppress large parts of their character, inclinations and abilities. These do not go away, they all form part of the shadow side of the character and they lie, hidden, deep in the recesses of every human person.

The word "shadow" can imply darkness and all the negative aspects of human character but to see it in this way is a mistake. The shadow represents all the unrecognized and unfulfilled sides of every person's character and this is likely to include many positive factors including virtues and abilities that have been suppressed and not recognized. **The shadow side grows in power the more it is not recognized.** Yet getting people to recognize and accept their shadow is a hard task. They may be more willing to accept the dark side of who they are than the many positive aspects of their character which have been suppressed as much as their negative characteristics.

Dreams

Like Freud, Jung attached great importance to dreams as he considered that dreams could give access to the unconscious mind and to the shadow side of a person. It can be worth recording your own dreams when you wake up and then trying to understand these – recognizing that all the characters in the dream in some way relate to yourself.

Imagine a seesaw – the task is to keep the seesaw in balance with both sides (the ego and the shadow) equally balanced. If the ego alone dominates then this may well make for success in the world but the whole unconscious side of the human being is ignored and this would have disastrous consequences later in life for the person. However to stand in the middle of a see-saw and keep one's balance one has to recognise that there are two ends to the see-saw – the ego and the shadow – and accepting the existence of the shadow is hard and something most people do not want to do.

Robert Johnson in "Owning your own shadow" portrays Jung's position through a medieval painting of the Tree of Life by Berthold Furtmeyer painted in 1481.

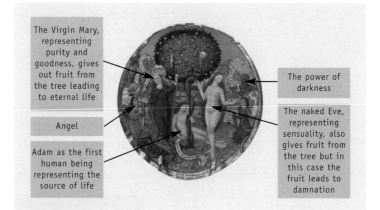

The Virgin Mary, representing purity and goodness, gives out fruit from the tree leading to eternal life

The power of darkness

Angel

The naked Eve, representing sensuality, also gives fruit from the tree but in this case the fruit leads to damnation

Adam as the first human being representing the source of life

Love

When we fall in love, we tend to project onto the loved one all that we see as best and most wonderful about human beings but, in fact, this is not the real person. Very often people are in love with the projections that they have created and relationships rapidly go wrong when the reality is realized. Love will only last if a person loves both the shadow side of the other and the conscious side and this is hard. It means loving all those features of another that he or she has repressed or is ashamed of or refuses to admit. If a person only loves their projection they will break the relationship once they realize that the other person is a person in their own right and does not represent the projection they have created.

Traditional Christian and Western thinking has seen the task of human beings as seeking to do good things in order to get to heaven and to avoid bad things in order to avoid hell. One should feel guilty about the bad things one does and give God credit for the all the good things. This is one way this picture can be interpreted. The saints are seen as those on the left because they are kind, virtuous and good and they will go to heaven, whereas the sinners are on the right because they are selfish, interested in physical pleasures (represented by the naked Eve and indicating the negative way in which sex has so often been interpreted in the Christian tradition) and reject goodness so they will go to hell.

However Jung, according to Johnson, considers this to be a mistaken understanding. The tree is the unity of human beings and every person is made up of two sides, ego and shadow. It is NOT the case that the ego is good and the shadow is all bad, the shadow is what has been repressed. The task of human life is to integrate the two sides. Guilt at the shadow is a waste of energy and unhelpful. Evil arises when the integration of ego and shadow does not happen and the shadow can then become terrible and forcefully destructive when it is ignored and suppressed. It will grow larger and larger until in the end it forces itself to the surface in some sudden and sometimes violent display of its power. This can then result in a sudden reversal so that the shadow side of a person,

Parents

Parents commonly project their own shadow onto their children by, for instance, pushing the children to do well at school because sub-consciously they themselves feel they have under-achieved. Parents try to live again through their children to realize their own dreams. By doing this, parents burden their children. There is a real sense in which this projection is the imposition of a dark unrecognized force which appears to have a life of its own.

which has been repressed for so long, suddenly takes control and forces a person to act in ways which friends and colleagues may consider inexplicable. This is, however, because the concealed shadow side has been ignored for so long that it demands attention by asserting itself.

Jung considered that unless individuals accept their shadow side it will assert itself either by achieving dominance or, in most cases, by projecting itself on others. Projection is vital for understanding Jung's psychology. People project many things onto others. For instance, feeling anger is part of being human but living in society we learn to suppress our anger and this then gets taken up by the shadow side – this shadow is then projected onto others and the person may accuse others of being angry. The person refuses to consciously recognize their own anger but the anger is revealed by its projection onto others.

Part of the path to overcoming evil lies in each person accepting their own shadow and refusing to let this dominate their actions. This means they have to recognise their shadow and accept it. Only by doing this can its power be overcome.

Each person in recognising their own shadow and its projections also has to accept that others will often project their shadow side onto them, and be willing to see and understand this and not to retaliate. This requires forgiveness and understanding of the actions of others rather than retaliation.

DOES PSYCHOLOGY SUCCEED?

Freud and Jung were key figures in a movement, which, in some quarters, has become incredibly popular. In some countries going to see your "shrink" is as commonplace as going to the supermarket. Having said this, it remains the privilege of a minority and, in the United States in particular, of those with money or good insurance. Various modern variations of psychotherapy have been developed, such as "constructivism"[1], in which the role of the psychotherapist is to help the individual to construct themselves in such a way that will enable them to cope with the world. People come to psychiatrists when they feel unable to live successfully in the world, and look for explanations in themselves; their early childhood or perhaps teenage years. The constructivist psychologist sees his or her task as being to help the person reconstruct a way of looking at the world which the person can substitute for their existing view, and which will enable them to cope successfully with the world. The key phrase here is "to cope successfully" and the issue of the truth and falsity of the constructed view does not arise in such an approach – all that matters is the psychological conditioning which will enable people to "cope successfully" and if this is achieved the constructivist psychologists will consider their task to be accomplished. Somewhat cynically this has been viewed as a way of turning unbearable neurosis into common unhappiness! It does not address questions of ultimate meaning and locates the source of people's unhappiness inside themselves rather than in disordered societies and cultures as well as in intolerable circumstances[2]. The central questions that have preoccupied the great thinkers of the world are ignored – is there a God? Am I a spiritual being? What is the source of evil? Is there a life after death? What is the difference between goodness and evil? are ignored. "Success in living in the world" is the only crucial factor and this means fitting in with the society in which one lives, which is not necessarily going to leave the individual feeling fulfilled.

The absence of a spiritual dimension in much modern day psychology finds its origin in Freud rather than in Jung. It is the natural consequence of the work of Freud in a post-modern society. All that matters is a pragmatic approach that keeps people away from depression and neurosis – rather like George Orwell's book 1984 – where the search for meaning and joy is replaced by obe-

---

[1] See What is Truth *(John Hunt Publishing 2003)* by Peter Vardy for a discussion of constructivism and its role in theories of truth.

[2] *See S Smail,* The Origins of Unhappiness *(Constable 1999)*

dience to "big brother". Many psychiatrists worked with the communist government in the Soviet Union and they saw their task as being to ensure that people conformed to the accepted world view of the government. In such an approach the nature of good and evil is defined in terms of conformity. Psychology has few, if any, insights into what it means to live a Good Life. In history, in films and in literature it is often those who refuse to accept the status quo and engage in a genuine search for truth and meaning outside of their own person and outside of their own selfish interests who find a joy and a peace available nowhere else. Historical examples might include the Buddha, Francis of Assisi, Ignatius of Loyola, Elizabeth Fry, Florence Nightingale, Ghandi, Nelson Mandela, Martin Luther King and many "ordinary" people who have lived simple, and apparently uneventful lives, quietly working to improve the lives of others. The inspiration for the work of these people is almost always a commitment to goodness and truth and a belief that these things do not lie solely in the individual psyche. In addition, all the great religions of the world claim that there is more to human fulfillment than life in the world.

QUESTIONS FOR CONSIDERATION

1. Can human beings be defined solely in terms of their actions?

2. Does Freud over-estimate the importance of inadequate development through his various sexual stages of childhood as the cause of evil behaviour?

3. Can you recognize the shadow side of either yourself or of any other person? How would you be able to identify the shadow side and why might recognizing it matter?

4. How might an explanation be given in psychological terms for someone who was passionately convinced that homosexuality was evil and wicked and that all homosexuals should be put in prison?

5. Why, psychologically, might the Virgin Mary be seen as an important figure in Christianity?

6. Do you think one can understand the nature of evil simply by understanding the way the human mind works?

CHAPTER ELEVEN

FREEDOM AND DETERMINISM

HARRY POTTER

The symbol of Slytherin house, one of the four houses at the boarding school, Hogwarts, which Harry Potter attends, is the snake and throughout the books the snake is seen as a symbol of evil. This draws on the ancient myth in the Hebrew and Christian scriptures of the story of the temptation of Adam and Eve by the snake. Slytherin was one of the original founders of Hogwarts who could speak to snakes and was interested in dark magic. The books make clear that magic can be used for good or evil purposes but in the final analysis it is the choice of individuals to decide for the good or evil side.

Harry potter with his owl Hedwig

At the beginning of his career at Hogwarts, Harry Potter has to go through the process that all new pupils at the school have to follow – and that is being sorted into houses by the "sorting hat". This is a very old, talking hat, which can look into the mind of each of the young students and decide where they will be best suited. Normally the hat makes its decision quickly, but in Harry's case it deliberates between Gryffindor and Slytherin. Harry could fit in well to both houses and the hat's initial reaction is that he would do well in Slytherin. He is intelligent and ambitious and Slytherin seems his natural home. Yet with every fibre of his being Harry keeps repeating whilst the hat is on his head and it is making its decision "NOT SLYTHERIN". The hat listens and he is put into Gryffindor. However he never forgets the hat's initial reaction and wonders whether the hat really thought he was evil after all. The "heir" of Slytherin, Lord Voldemort, tried to kill Harry Potter when he was a baby and instead had many of his powers taken from him. In many ways Harry is similar to Lord Voldemort, for example he can speak to snakes, and gradually Harry comes to realize this.

At the end of the second book Harry discusses this concern with Professor Dumbledore who replies:

"The sorting hat put you in Gryffindor. Listen to me Harry. You happen to have many qualities Salazar Slytherin prized ... his own very rare gift, parceltongue [an ability to speak to snakes], resourcefulness, determination, a certain disregard for rules ... Yet the sorting hat placed you in Gryffindor. You know why that was. Think."

"It only put me in Gryffindor because I asked not to go in Slytherin." Harry replied.

"Exactly!" said Dumbledore, *"which makes you very different from Tom Riddle [the young Voldemort]. It is our choices which show what we truly are far more than our abilities."*

This issue is at the heart of the debate about freedom. Human choices are decisive. Different people may have different abilities but it is the question of whether they are free to choose how to use these potentialities for good or evil that is central to the debate. If humans have no freedom then the very idea of human responsibility for good and evil disappears. If humans are free, as the Harry Potter books suggest, and as human experience suggests, then they are responsible for their actions and can be held accountable. It is this that this chapter will address.

THE PROBLEM

Sometimes philosophy is about taking very simple statements and analysing them to see how complex they really are. Take the statement "I can X" where X is some task. There are many alternatives:

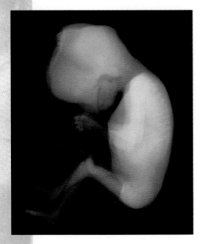

A foetus has the potential to develop into a baby, into a child and then into an adult.

1. *I can read a book*

2. *I can study hard*

3. *I can drink a cup of coffee*

4. *I can walk to the park*

5. *I can steal*

6. *I can lie*

7. *I can gossip*

Most of us can (and sometimes do) say these statements and mean them. Of course, if we are disabled and in a wheelchair then we cannot say "I can walk to the park". Also there are some things we clearly cannot do for instance "I cannot fly unaided" and "I cannot live for ever". These latter statements indicate limits to our powers based on our human nature and the laws of the world in which we live. They indicate that there are many things that we clearly cannot do. We have limited control of our bodies – we have to eat, drink and breathe or we will die. We have to excrete waste products. We have to grow from a foetus to a baby to a child to a teenager and to an adult. We have to grow old and die. It may be that we would like to avoid some of these things but we cannot. Our human nature sets clear limits to what we can do. Yet even when these limits are clearly recognized, this still leaves open a wide range of possibilities and when we say "I can X" what we are doing is to say that X is amongst the range of possible things which we can do.

So far this is straightforward, however the real problems start to arise when we look at the "I can X" statement in more detail. It is one thing to say that I am capable of doing X, but is this the same thing as saying I am capable of not doing X? To put it another way, does:

1. "I can X"

necessarily require us to say:

2. "I can choose not to X"

This raises the whole issue of whether or not human beings are free and this is vital to the problem of evil. There is no question that it would have been true in 1936 if someone has said:

"The Nazis could murder six million Jews.".

However terrible it is to recognize that human beings are capable of doing this, we know that they are. We can also say the same of many other evils said before the events happened:

1. *"Stalin can kill more than two million of his own people"*

2. *"Pol Pot in Cambodia can kill 1.5 million people"*

3. *"Brothers can bully sisters"*

4. *"Husbands can commit adultery"*

5. *"Students can cheat"*

6. *"Girls can dump their boyfriends"*

We know these statements are true. These things are, indeed, within the range of possibilities available to human beings. Most people would say that the people who do these things are wrong, even if not everyone would describe cheating, adultery or bullying as evil and perhaps girls dumping their boyfriends is not even wrong. Evil things, then, can be done by human beings.

However the really important question is whether human beings can choose NOT to do these things. Most people would immediately say "of course they can", but it is not as simple as that.

The issue is highly important for any discussion of evil as if people cannot prevent themselves from doing something, then they would generally not be regarded as morally responsible.

Scientists have produced a "robo-rat" a real, live, radio controlled rat which can be directed forwards and backwards, left and right and up and down just like a radio controlled car. Electrodes are implanted in the brain of the rat and these are attached to a tiny transmitter on the rat's back. The human operator can see where the rat goes through a miniature camera strapped to its back and can direct the rat wherever the operator wishes it to go. The rat,

- Charlotte can do what she wants to do

- Charlotte can do what she thinks is right

- Charlotte can do what she feels like doing

- Charlotte is not prevented by any external forces from doing as she wishes

- Charlotte has the power to do as she would like

- If Charlotte wanted she could do something different from what she presently wants to do

NONE OF THESE STATEMENTS MEAN THAT A PERSON IS FREE. If you look at them carefully they could all be compatible with someone thinking that they were free but actually being completely determined. For instance:

- What Charlotte WANTS to do may be completely determined by her background, or

- What she feels like doing may simply be a product of her psychological conditioning, which she cannot control.

clearly, has no choice but to go where the operator decides – it is effectively a robot. Are human beings like this?

Determinists maintain that everything that a human being does is determined. They are determined by social factors, psychological factors and by events in the past. The determinist claims that although there are many things that a human being can do, in fact there are just as many things that they are incapable of **not** doing. If enough was known about a person's psychological make-up and sociological background we would be able to predict their behaviour. Choices, which appear to be made freely, are actually completely determined by these factors. The individual may not be aware of these factors.

Every human being is influenced by many factors in their past including:

1. Genetic make up. This determines height, weight, appearance, gender, perhaps sexual preferences, athletic ability, propensity to disease and many other factors.

2. Parental influence. The influence of parents is tremendous, particularly in the early years. Whether or not a baby was cuddled, talked to, left to cry, smacked, abused, severely disciplined, etc will have tremendous effects later in life. Also the social conditioning that comes from parents will influence the child.

3. School life. Whether a person was bullied, a failure, part of the "in group", spotty, lonely, physically attractive or unattractive all have a great effect.

The more we learn about human beings, the more it appears that much of what they do is determined by factors over which they have no control. This supports the theory of DETERMINISM, which holds that human beings are not free at all since everything they do is determined. If determinism is true, then human beings are not free. There is no way to prove determinism false as, although a person may act contrary to all expectation the determinist can still say, "Ah, that is because we are still ignorant. We do not know all the factors, if we did we would have been able to predict this behaviour."

If determinism is right, then it would seem that talk of good and evil actions is meaningless as if every person is determined to act as they do and if they cannot act otherwise, then there is no difference between good and evil. Of course most people would say that Mother Teresa was good and that Hitler was evil, but if both of them were completely determined, then morally they were the same. Neither is morally praiseworthy or blameworthy, as they were incapable of acting otherwise.

Immanuel Kant recognised that human free will could not be proven, but he held that non-determined freedom HAD to be assumed as it was necessary for humans to be free to act for there to be any discussion of morality at all. If every human being is a programmed robot, then talk of right or wrong, virtue and vice, good and evil are meaningless – all they might indicate is our emotional attitude to certain actions and even these emotions would be determined!

To what extent does parental and social conditioning determine who we shall become?

Some philosophers hold that it is possible BOTH to be free AND to be determined. They hold this because they maintain that there are two different understandings of what it means to talk of freedom:

• *A NON-COMPATIBILIST is someone who maintains that human beings cannot both be free and be wholly determined. If humans are free then they are not wholly determined and if they are wholly determined then they are not free. It is important to recognize that a non-compatibilist would certainly consider that human beings are influenced by genetics, education etc however they would deny that humans are controlled by these factors. There is a significant element of freedom.*

• *A COMPATIBILIST is someone who maintains that human beings can be both free and determined. They maintain that freedom is defined as the ability to do what a person wishes to do, free from external constraint. Human beings have, they claim, this freedom, but this does not prevent them also being determined by internal genetic, psychological and other factors. Charlotte can therefore do what she wants to do but what she wants to do is wholly determined.*

In order to have a discussion which maintains that humans are responsible for the evil they do it is necessary to assume that human beings have non-determined freedom – in other words it is necessary to be a non-compatibilist.

Another challenge to freedom can be presented, however, and this is to say that there

Imagine

Imagine that you perform an action X – it can be anything you like: getting a cup of coffee, going for a walk, speaking to someone you care for, writing a letter. Why did you do this action? There may be many reasons – in the case of getting a cup of coffee you may be thirsty, you normally have a coffee break at this time, you are bored with this book and want a break, a friend has asked you to have a coffee. Each of these reasons could be explored in more detail and so the process continues. The determinist will maintain that if we knew enough ALL the causes that lead us to act as we do can be worked out and, although we do not like to think in these terms, in fact we are completely determined.

The alternative, say the determinists, is to claim that getting the coffee was just a random action, without any explanation at all.

are only two alternatives when it comes to human actions. Either:

1. Behaviour can be explained by genetics, childhood, psychological factors and sociological factors

2. They are random acts with no explanation at all.

Philosophers who take this view hold that if actions are not caused by who a person is and if this is not determined by all the past things that have happened to him or her, then the only alternative is to claim that the actions are random. Random actions are not caused, but neither – it is held – can they be used to make someone morally accountable.

This is where another term enters the discussion that is rather more complicated – that is **ORIGINATION.** To say of A that it is the ORIGIN of B, is to say that A can explain B. For instance, in Christianity, Islam and Judaism God is considered to be the origin of the created universe. God explains the created universe and God's decision to create it is the only reason for the universe existing. To say of God that God is the originating cause is to say that it was God's deliberate choice that caused the universe – it was not a random action.

Freedom and moral praise or blame depends on human beings being **ORIGINATING AGENTS** – in other words they are the origin of the acts that they perform. Whilst they may clearly be influenced by their past, nevertheless at the point of the action they have a freedom to act or not to act.

No one quite understands why a person acts as he does. There seem to be two alternatives but a third is needed!

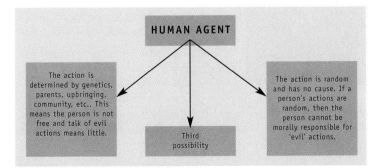

HUMAN AGENT

The action is determined by genetics, parents, upbringing, community, etc.. This means the person is not free and talk of evil actions means little.

Third possibility

The action is random and has no cause. If a person's actions are random, then the person cannot be morally responsible for 'evil' actions.

ORIGINATION claims that there is a third possibility – namely that humans are originating causes of their actions and, whilst they may be influenced by the past and may at times be unpredictable, nevertheless human actions are NEITHER determined NOR are they random. **Origination holds that there are no laws, material or psychological, which determine how a human being will act and that each individual has a power to decide how to act.** This is not an easy idea to justify and, indeed, many philosophers would reject it, but the universal human experience is that, no matter how many influences there may be on human actions, nevertheless we do have free will. If this experience is reliable then people are morally responsible and accountable for their actions. In other words whilst philosophers may be unable to explain it, human experience is strongly on the side of human beings being ORIGINATING AGENTS.

Immanuel Kant held that as human beings are made up of matter, there must be some explanation for human freedom that is not material. The human capacity to act as originating causes must be non-physical since everything in the material universe is either subject to natural laws or is random. This means that human beings, if they are to be free, must have some form of metaphysical or spiritual basis which provides the possibility for free action.

Take this picture of a feather in the air. What causes it to behave as it does? There may be many answers including:

1. That it fell from a bird during a fight with a cat

2. That there is no rain to keep it on the ground

3. That the wind is blowing

4. That the wind caused by a passing car swept it in the air from the pavement where it fell

5. That the weight of the feather is low and therefore gravity cannot quickly bring it to earth and the wind can blow it easily

We may not know all the causes but the determinist would say that, in principle, all the causes could be known and a full explanation could be given for the feather's movement.

Are human beings like feathers blown this way and that and acting from causes that we only dimly understand? The feather has no freedom to act on its own and neither, say the determinists, do human beings. Animals are like feathers only the causes of their actions are more complex and human being are simply even more complex animals. If this is the case then evil exists as part of a vast, determined universe. To claim that humans are originating causes is to reject this view – it is to claim that, unlike a feather, although human beings are influenced by many external factors they can nevertheless make their own non-determined decisions.

Take the following example of the decision to murder an innocent person:

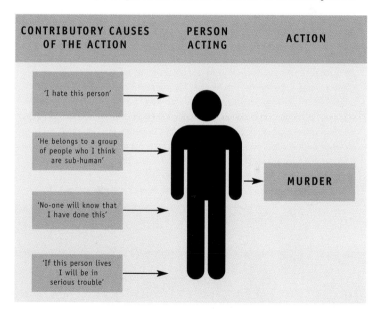

If the contributory causes do not determine the person to act, then the act appears to be a random act (and then the person acting is not responsible). The alternative is to claim that the person acting is an ORIGINATING CAUSE and, whilst he/she may be influenced by the contributory causes of the action, it is he/she who makes the final decision and must therefore accept responsibility for what he/she did.

Tenzin Palmo

Tenzin Palmo was a British girl who grew up above a fish and chip shop in the East End of London. In her early 20s she traveled to Northern India and, after long years of solitary meditation and training, become a Buddhist monk.

"The reason we are not enlightened is because we are lazy. There's no other reason. We do not bother to bring ourselves back to the present because we are too fascinated by the games the mind is playing. If one genuinely thinks about Renunciation, it is not a giving up of external things like money, leaving home or one's family. That's easy. Genuine renunciation is giving up our fond thoughts, all our delight in memories, hopes and daydreams, our mental chatter. To renounce that and stay naked in the present, that is renunciation. The thing is, we say we want to be Enlightened but we don't really. Only bits of us want to be enlightened. The ego, which thinks how nice, comfortable and pleasant it would be. But to really drop everything and go for it! We could do it in a moment but we don't do it. And the reason is we are too lazy. We are stopped by fear and lethargy – the great inertia of the mind. The practice is there. Anyone on the Buddhist path certainly knows these things. So how is it we are not enlightened? We have no one to blame but ourselves. This is why we stay in Samsara because we always find excuses. Instead we should wake ourselves up. The whole Buddhist path is about waking up. Yet the desire to keep sleeping is so strong. However much we say we will awake in order to help all sentient beings we don't really want to. We like dreaming."
(Tenzin Palmo, quoted in *The Cave in the Snow* by Vickie MacKenzie p.172)

Silence and stillness can contribute to human beings taking control of their minds and thus achieving freedom

FREEDOM - NOT BLACK AND WHITE

The debate between determinists and those who take a libertarian view of freedom is often presented in black and white terms – people support one or the other. Perhaps, however, it is not like this. Perhaps, instead, freedom is an achievement, something that human beings are capable of coming to after a long, hard struggle. In the previous chapter some theories of human psychological development were outlined. Psychology is still in its infancy and we are far from clear on what influences or controls human actions. What is clear, however, is that the psychological roots of actions are deep and far from properly understood. Freedom may only be possible once each individual has come to some understanding, however incomplete, of the psychological forces acting on him or her. Arguably it is perhaps only once these forces are understood that a person can claim to be free and to have mastery over themselves. The Buddhist tradition would support this view – the first stage to freedom is the understanding of the self. Only then can the hard road be undertaken which may bring a person to begin to control their own mind and, thereby, to begin to achieve freedom. Perhaps it is only when this is done that human beings can begin to control their evil inclinations.

QUESTIONS FOR CONSIDERATION

1. What are the main factors that you consider limit your freedom? What factors might there be, of which you are not conscious, that control the way you behave?

2. Do you consider that you are free to decide who to love? How might one argue for and against this claim?

3. Why might Buddhists claim that most human beings are lazy?

4. Do you consider that, in principle, it will one day be possible to predict all human behaviour?

5. Is freedom something that is achieved or do all people have it?

CHAPTER TWELVE

INSTITUTIONAL EVIL

"All college students are being asked to sign an official statement to the effect that they 'sympathize with the Germans and approve of the New Order'. Eighty percent have decided to obey the dictates of their conscience, but the penalty will be severe. Any student refusing to sign will be sent to a German labour camp." Anne Frank's Diary May 18, 1943 referring to events in Amsterdam

Where is real evil to be found? With the devil or Satan? In the human psyche? In an absence of God? Increasingly, it may be claimed that evil resides in institutions. Institutions seem to have a life of their own. Institutions have rules and regulations, both written and unwritten. To work in an institution means being fully absorbed into the ethos of the institution and believing that the way the organization works is the only way that it can work. Change is regarded as rather threatening: "This is the way it has always been done, why change now?" Change will be regarded with heavy suspicion and resisted, because to accept change would be to admit that the way things "have always been done" was not the best way. Those who wish for change may be regarded as troublemakers. They may feel that they risk their job if they "stir things up" too much, even if their proposals are for the common good. Individuals work as part of the machinery of the institution, and although they may be encouraged to think that they are invaluable, they are replaceable. It feels as though the institution controls those who work in them. Institutions vary in character and size – from the local cricket club to large public services.

156

Everyone is subjected to a variety of influences as they grow up. People have the traditions and values of their own homes, but there are many other influences that a person is subjected to through television, schools and the communities within which they are brought up. Everybody is brought up in a particular country, and will almost sub-consciously learn to abide by the rules, both written and unwritten of that particular country. In England the tradition of forming a queue has a strong heritage and is obeyed with great formality at bus stops and post offices and in all shops. Waiting your turn is part of British culture. Elsewhere in the world this is far from the case and pushing or queue jumping is normal. In the United States "American values" and "free-

To defeat evil it is first necessary to locate it

dom" as well as the importance of the American flag are almost unquestioned. Equally the formation of a person into a particular set of religious beliefs (or otherwise) and their acceptance of all sorts of macro issues, such as political and economic structures, happens unaided by formal education. To a large extent these ideals and ideas are absorbed and will determine the individual's attitudes. The individual who challenges these accepted norms will be rare.

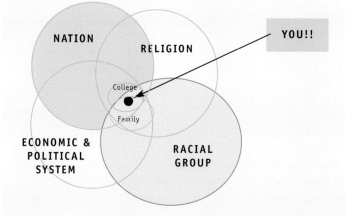

The 19th-century British philosopher, F H Bradley, developed this idea and suggested that without all of these influences the individual is virtually nothing at all. Bradley maintained that human beings were educated into all moral duties and obligations by their culture and the institutions that they were influenced by. He put the position cogently in a chapter of his book *Ethical Studies* entitled "My Station and its duties". Bradley maintains that a person:

"... is what he is because he is a born and educated social being, and a member of an individual social organism; that if you make an abstraction of all this, this is the same in him and in others, what you have left is not an Englishman, nor a man, but some I know not what residuum ...."

In other words, apart from the community that forms the individual people are nothing. Throughout the modern world, decisions and policies are not made by individual decision makers, but by institutions – these are the policies and decisions of governments, non-governmental organizations, multinational companies and the like.

Multi-national companies are institutions with enormous power and influence upon the modern world because they are VERY rich. Their revenue is often larger than the income of whole countries.

LARGEST COMPANIES IN THE WORLD BY 2001 REVENUE

Company	Country of Origin	2001 Revenue	Comparison
1) Wal-Mart	US	$219 182m	Size of Sweden
2) Exxon/Mobile	US	$191 581m	Larger than Turkey
3) General Motors	US	$177 260m	Larger than Denmark
4) Ford Motor	US	$162 412m	Larger than Poland
5) Daimler/Chrysler	Germany	$149 608m	Larger than Norway
6) Royal Dutch Shell	NL/Britain	$149 146m	Larger than Norway
7) BP	Britain	$148 062m	Larger than Norway
8) Enron (bankrupt 2002)	US	$138 718m	Larger than South Africa
9) Mitsubishi	Japan	$126 629m	Larger than Finland
10) General Electric	US	$125 913m	Larger than Greece

It can be argued that the real evils in the world come from INSTITUTIONAL EVIL – in other words evils due to institutions that act in each country and throughout the world. There are many examples of this "evil" at work in institutions:

a) *In Britain London's Metropolitan police force and in the United States the Los Angeles police force have both been accused of institutional evil. In particular they have been accused of racism – racism it was said was so deeply rooted in both organizations that it was a part of the very fabric of the organization. Nobody questioned racism, because it was the way it had always been.*

b) *The sales of the world's top 200 companies are 18 times higher than the total annual income of the world's 1.2 billion poorest people.*

c) *The wealthiest 1% of the world's population receive as much total income as the poorest 57%. Eleven million children under the age of five die needlessly every year due to poverty. Britain spends more on pet food that it's entire expenditure on aid to the Third World. More than a quarter of the world's population do not have access to permanent, clean drinking water. They live in poverty and many children will not go to school and will have to start work at a very early age. Many people have no medical care at all and death in childbirth and in infancy is common. Many people would attribute this to institutional evil.*

Companies around the world spend million of pounds/franks/deutchmarks and dollars to ensure that governments support what they do. The following are the latest available figures for expenditure on lobbying in the united states.

TOTAL REGISTERED EXPENDITURE BY US INDUSTRY ON LOBBYING

(Persuading governments, the media and others to support their policies)
US $1 176 975 243

TOTAL POLITICAL CAMPAIGN CONTRIBUTIONS TO POLITICAL PARTIES

(Persuading politicians to support the company policies or to secure orders)
US $552 556 068

d) The governments in many of the poorer countries are corrupt and instead of working to help their own people, politicians are interested in making money for themselves. Within these countries this is an accepted way of working. Corruption, such as demanding and offering bribes, is normal. The people in these countries accept their institutions and to challenge them would be dangerous. Other countries conspire to keep them in power because it is in their interests to do so. Western countries regularly support corrupt regimes that do not care for their own people because these regimes support the policies of Western companies.

e) The level of giving by countries in the Western world for the benefit of the poorest countries is incredibly low. Twenty years ago the United Nations recommended that Western countries give 1% of their gross national budget to the poorest countries in the world. Hardly any countries achieve this objective and the percentage of giving by, for instance, the United States and Britain and been continually decreasing over the years. The populations of Western countries are reluctant to see more money given to poor countries and consistently vote against any attempt to increase overseas aid. A government that promised to increase overseas aid by any significant margin would not be voted into power. The institutions of democracy demand that the government is elected, and this means that overseas aid is not high on

The institutions which keep many people in poverty are often 'faceless' and hard to identify

the list of government priorities, because the voters want a higher standard of living for themselves. The almost universally unchallenged acceptance, in Western countries, of judging the value of a person by their financial strength is partly to blame for this.

f) The institutional demand of Western governments to control their own budgets and not to form any kind of "world government" which would take responsibility for world issues, such as poverty and environmental issues, is a contribution factor to institutional evil.

g) Rules and regulations within Western dominated financial institutions for the provision of loans to the Third World is another area where these bodies stand accused of institutional evil. In particular the World Bank imposes harsh conditions on some poor countries that take loans. This sometimes means that these countries stop producing food that their own people can eat and instead produce "cash crops", such as tobacco or coffee which can be sold overseas and produce the funds needed to pay back the loans. Also the privatisation of essential services in Third World countries often means that basic necessities are placed out of reach of the poor.

h) Oxfam estimates that international companies who set up factories to make goods in poor countries – because the labour is cheap - use "creative accounting" to reduce on paper the amount of profit that they make. This means that the international company does not pay the right amount of tax to the developing country. It is estimated that poor countries lose tax revenues of $50 BILLION per year in this way. "Creative accounting" is an accepted institution in the Western world.

i) The world trade order is, many hold, corrupt because it is controlled by the

---

An exercise

1) Write down all the groups, communities and organizations to which you belong or of which you form part.

2) Then list what attitudes or types of behaviour these groups encourage which "everyone" accepts and yet which members of some other groups would reject.

3) Name these other groups and consider why they might consider any of the attitudes of the groups to which you belong to be evil or wicked.

4) If you had been brought up as they have been brought up, would you agree with them?

5) What, apart from the accident of birth, makes your behaviour "right" and their judgment of your behaviour "wrong"?

The pollution in the affluent West is, many scientists hold, partly responsible for global climate change which affects the poor most

wealthy Western countries and the institutions that regulate the world trade system (such as GATT – the General Agreement on Tariffs and Trade) insist on free trade. This opens the markets of poor countries to Western competition and yet the West does not always honour the principle of free trade when its own industries might be threatened. For example the West closes its markets to things such as "finished" products or cheap agricultural products or steel. Poor countries are forced, therefore, to sell raw materials at low prices and to buy finished goods at Western prices. They are not allowed to sell raw materials such as steel or farm produce because this would undermine the Western market.

j) Some companies, in order to reduce costs, produce goods in poor countries and insist that workers (often children) work very long hours at very low pay and with few holidays or medical care entitlements. This type of institutional evil would not be tolerated in Western countries.

k) The World Bank, working within the institution of capitalism, has pushed many governments in poor countries to privatise water supplies. Water, instead of being a basic right, is a commodity to be sold at a profit to those who can afford it.

l) The whole of planet earth is threatened by a global crisis caused by *pollution. The Western countries produce far more pollution than poorer ones yet their institutions mean that action to reduce pollution is made very difficult. In the United States it is almost an institution to drive a large car, even for short distances. A person's status is judged partly on the car they drive. The oil companies are very powerful and any challenges which might threaten levels of consumption of petrol are powerfully lobbied against. The United States has refused to ratify the Kyoto treaty which set limits on pollution. The result is that many other countries will refuse to co-operate against pollution and the planet itself is threatened.*

m) *The institutions of free trade and capitalism combine together sometimes to create the potential for great evil. Supported by these institutions defence companies push very hard to sell weapons to countries which (a). cannot afford these weapons (b). have a population that needs food and water, education and medical resources far more than weapons. People are in desperate poverty. In Tanzania, some of whose people are starving, an advanced military radar system was ordered, which it did not need, partly, it is suspected, due to bribes being paid and also because those in power and arms companies wanting the deal to go through. The danger is not only that the people of Tanzania continue to go hungry but also that the countries around Tanzania will wonder what Tanzania plans to do with its advanced war machinery. Feeling threatened by Tanzania they could also try to buy similar goods. This necessarily increases the gap between rich and poor but sickeningly it also adds to the risk of war in these poor areas. War, when it happens, not only means death but the consequence of war is even greater poverty. It is the institution of capitalism which demands that arms producers make a profit, and free trade means that these companies are free to find markets outside of their own country. Together these institutions create the potential for the evil of arms trading.*

The key point in institutional evil is that people seldom notice it, people are seldom aware of it because "that is the way the world is". No one challenges the status quo or makes a stand against the evils in the institutions of which they form a part. Worse than this, however, even if people do become aware of being part of a structure that is unjust or evil, they may well feel impotent to do anything about it. The problems can seem so large and the possibility of bringing about any change can seem so difficult that it is very easy for people just to give up and to consider that it is not their business.

Most people willingly participate in the structures within which they have been born and commit themselves to these structures with passion and conviction – certain that they are right and others are wrong. This view is seldom based on analysis or careful thought; instead it is a matter of habit.

Support for nationalism provides, perhaps, a clear example. If a country goes to war, almost everyone in the country supports the government of the country and the national war effort. This applied in the great World Wars between Germany and the Allies, in the war between Iran and Iraq and even in what President Bush described as the war against terrorism. Almost without exception, US citizens consider that the United States was in the right in waging war against the government of Afghanistan (the Taliban) and that those who carried out the September 11 attacks were evil fanatics. On the streets of most Islamic cities across the Arab world, it was the United States who was viewed as evil and those who carried out the attacks were regarded as heroes, who gave their lives in a noble cause. All too rarely do the citizens of any country sit down and really try to understand both sides. Nationalism gets in the way. Patriotism and "the flag" can be used to encourage support for the worst forms of evil – those in which other people are simply regarded as "other" and somehow less than worthy of human dignity and respect

The same can apply with institutional evil within corporate life. Companies may behave in morally reprehensible ways and this is

Evil in common activity

MUCH EVIL IS DONE BY ORDINARY PEOPLE IN THEIR ORDINARY LIVES:

Hannah Arendt, in her often-quoted account of the trial of Nazi Adolf Eichmann, *In Jerusalem: A Report on the Banality of Evil*, wrote: "The deeds were monstrous, but the doer was quite ordinary, commonplace, and neither demonic or monstrous." Arendt concluded that Eichmann, far from intending to do evil, sent thousands to their deaths merely because of "a lack of imagination" and because he wanted to get promotion. His only motive was personal advancement: "he never realized what he was doing."

THE LAW AS A SOURCE OF EVIL

Judge Richard A Posner of the Seventh United States Circuit Court of Appeals is regarded as one of the most intelligent and thoughtful judges in the US. Posner wrote on the subject of evil in an essay (reviewing Ingo Muller's book, *Hitler's Justice*) entitled "Courting Evil" in *The New Republic*. Posner claims that the German judiciary did evil because it "was so immersed in a professional culture as to be oblivious to the human consequences of their decisions". Judge Posner asked in this essay whether American "prosecutors who pursue marijuana growers, sellers of dirty magazines, and violators of arcane campaign financing regulations are inappropriately using their offices in much the same manner as did prosecutors who earlier brought charges against Germans for 'dishonouring the race'." Posner urged judges against being "eager enlisters in the popular movements of the day". His point is that judges often just go along with popular opinion in their society – this is what the judges in Nazi Germany did, it is what judges in Stalin's Russia did and it is what many Western judges do. They may be respectable people but due to lack of thought they may be the authors of evil.

EVIL AS APPLYING THE RULES

Sometimes strict application of the rules or the law can result in evil. Kevin Hogan was a model citizen. He bought a fishing boat for $140 000 and headed with a crew of three to fish off the coast of Alaska. Engine problems forced the boat into a Canadian port and the Canadian customs searched the boat. They found 1.7 grams of marijuana in the jacket of one of the crew. Customs officials accepted that Hogan knew nothing about the marijuana. Under the "Zero Tolerance" program initiated less than two months earlier, even small amounts of drugs could result in arrests and forfeitures of property. Customs agents decided to seize Hogan's boat. Hogan had planned to use the boat during Alaska's 24-hour halibut season later that month. The seizure of his

Evil in common activity (Contd)

boat meant he could not pay back the mortgage on it and lost the $110 000 he had spent 15 years saving. More than a 1000 people signed a petition saying this was unfair but the Canadian customs insisted that it was just obeying the rules.

RIGIDITY AS PRODUCING EVIL

After the events of September 11, 2001 in New York, President Bush proclaimed a war against the evil of terrorism. This was very popular and had massive public support. In Kansas, an 18-year-old boy was driving his car and stopped at a railway crossing, got out of his car and chatted to another driver. The boy said he was looking forward to going to a school dance but was not sure if his parents would let him go. He is reported to have said: "If they don't let me go to the prom, I may have to blow up the school." The driver reported the boy's comment to police, who arrested him and searched his home. They found no evidence that he had ever considered making a bomb, he had no equipment and no knowledge of how to proceed but he was charged with "making a terroristic threat against school officials or a school". This was a new law introduced after school shootings, which carries a 10-year prison sentence.

(These examples are taken from the University of Missouri/Kansas web site)

generally accepted because no one in the organization queries it. If anyone does raise questions then they will probably be told that:

a) *"Everyone" carries out the behaviour in question,*

b) *If the company did not do it someone else would,*

c) *Jobs depend on getting the contract or carrying out the behaviour that the questionable actions are intended to achieve, and*

d) *If the person concerned persists in raising questions, this could have a negative effect on their promotion possibilities or even their job.*

This last is a none too subtle threat which makes institutional evil so common. The institution ensures compliance by threatening any who dissent – the threats are often covert, but they are still present. Racism and sexism are common in many police forces simply because the whole culture of certain police forces, the male bonding involved in meeting dangerous situations and a history of police who were largely male and white encourages racism and sexism. The climate is such that it is almost impossible for young recruits to speak out against the prevailing institutional evil and they soon find that they have accepted it and participate fully in it.

In the same way the unity within a nation or culture, the constant media pressure to conform to the country's way of seeing the world (different political parties within a country seldom disagree about the country's perception of its place in the world) almost always ensures that nationalism is a powerful bonding force. In fact it can be argued that of all the evils of the last two hundred years, nationalism is the greatest – it is this that ensures that when a country goes to war almost everyone (except for a tiny minority of pacifists) supports the war effort. Loyalty to country is a powerful bonding force – in America young people are constantly taught loyalty to "the flag" (since there is no king or queen to provide a focus of unity above politics, the flag serves as a good alternative). "The American way" is taught as being unquestionably right and the idea that these institutions might at times be evil and oppressive is barely considered.

Frequently religious institutions can perpetuate institutional evil by ensuring compliance of their members with the accepted state of affairs. A few examples can help to illustrate this:

- *For many years the "divine right of kings" was maintained by the Catholic Church. Any resistance to the king was held to be a sin and to ensure damnation. The king*

Harry Potter

In the Harry Potter books, the cleaning and cooking at Hogwarts School is done entirely by house elves. These elves work unseen in the kitchens and come out at night to clean. No one even notices the work that they do – food appears as if by magic and the castle is always clean. These house elves are highly intelligent but they are not paid, they get no holidays and they cannot leave their employers. Most of the rich magicians' families have house elves who do all the housework in the home – no one notices them or pays any attention to them.

It takes the young Hermione to recognize that these elves are kept in conditions of near slavery and she begins a campaign to free them – insisting that they should be paid and have holidays and be free to leave those they work for if they wish to do so. All her friends make fun of her and she is something of a figure of ridicule because everyone says that the elves are happy and it is their task in life to cook and clean. Hermione will not have this and takes a stand against what she sees as the institutional evil in her school. This takes great courage as it is a lonely stand and she gets almost no support – but it is only by the willingness of individuals to take such stands that institutional evil may be overcome.

was accountable to God alone: non-resistance and obedience to the monarch was enjoined by the law of God. Blind obedience to those in authority was thus supported by the church.

- Pope *Leo X condemned Martin Luther for saying that burning heretics at the stake was against the will of God. Pope Leo's teaching was officially the magisterium's position until 1966 when the Second Vatican Council excluded the burning of heretics. Many countries excluded the burning of heretics long before it became official church teaching (this is argued by Bernard Hoose of Heythrop College, University of London). Put simply, the teachings of Pope Leo X were wrong but for many years the institution supported execution by burning for those who disagreed with the Church.*

- *Many generations of Popes specifically sanctioned the persecution and oppression of the Jews. The concentration camps of Nazi Germany were not isolated instances – they were the culmination of continual oppression of the Jewish people by the Christian Church, with popes, bishops and the magisterium often taking the lead.*

There is nothing wrong with being in error – human institutions err and they are certainly not infallible. What is called "Institutional Evil" arises when these institutions (be they state, religious grouping, society, ethnic grouping or club) no longer recognize the possibility that they may be mistaken and instead coerce and enforce their own view without regard to the possibility that they could be mistaken. Institutional evil is possible in any organization. It can happen in any nation, cultural group, commercial organization, church, family or when any group is so certain that it has the truth or that issues of truth and justice do not matter that it uses its power to prevent people raising questions and challenging the status quo.

The Lord of the Rings is a struggle between good and evil communities yet the role of the individual is central

If there is such a thing as institutional evil, with whom does the responsibility lie? Does the institution take on a life of its own with evil lurking in dark corners waiting for the unwary writer of policy to pass it by and be taken under its power? Is institutional evil like possessing one of the rings in the *Lord of the Rings*, virtually unavoidable? Or is the evil allowed to creep in and given permission to grow by management and ordinary people too?

Martin Niemöller, the great German protestant theologian who was arrested by the Nazis before finally escaping to the United States said:

"When Hitler attacked the Jews I was not a Jew, therefore I was not concerned. And when Hitler attacked the Catholics, I was not a Catholic, and therefore, I was not concerned. And when Hitler attacked the unions and the industrialists, I was not a member of the unions and I was not concerned. Then Hitler attacked me and the Protestant church — and there was nobody left to be concerned."

The Jewish theologian Martin Buber discussed the nature of evil in his book *Good and Evil* and rejected the traditional idea that evil and good are two separate poles. Buber argued that evil is not, as it is commonly understood, the opposite of good:

"It is usual to think of good and evil as two poles, two opposite directions, the antithesis of one another. We must begin by doing away with this convention."

Buber argued that good comes from a dedication to walking the moral path, from carefully seeking in all one's actions to do what is right. Evil by contrast, occurs not simply when one does something wrong but from a person failing to give attention to what is right. Goodness only occurs when a person works at being good and attends very closely to the difficult task of being good. Evil, by contrast, happens because of a failure to attend to the good. In a way, evil is then a natural state because a person just happens to be evil whereas striving is needed in order to be good.

Institutional evil is probably the most prevalent and common evil in existence today and yet most people do not even realize that it exists. In order to even begin to recognize it, there is a need to stand completely outside the framework in which one lives and which everyone accepts. This is not only exceptionally hard to do but is also a lonely position to be in. To challenge the values of one's own nation, community and family is hard. Most people consider that it is right and good to support one's own nation, community and family. However if the values held are wrong then supporting them is also wrong. Any nation, organization or group that has values that damage others is guilty of institutional evil.

What is most challenging of all is that those who think they are being good and virtuous may actually be contributing to institutional evil. They may be told by their friends and family how good they are, they may be praised by the society and community in which they live but they may actually be acting in ways that cause suffering and they may be contributors to evil.

1. *Those who were part of the German SS and those who contributed to the killing of millions under Stalin's Government in Russia, were looked up to by their families and friends, praised by their communities and given medals by their country – yet they were the agents of evil.*

2. *Employees of large corporate banks may be respectable, church going people but they may actually be contributing to the untold suffering and misery of hundreds of thousands of people, they may be the agents of evil.*

3. *Members of military forces that carry out the orders they've been given faithfully and well, with courage and dedication, may be instruments of institutional evil.*

4. *Judges and lawyers who maintain and contribute to an unjust system may be contributors to institutional evil.*

5. *Taxpayers who finance governments who act in their name may be contributors to institutional evil because if it was not for the money paid in taxes the government could not continue.*

6. *Dedicated members of a religious group who remain faithful to its teaching may be contributing to the suppression of dissidents, women, minorities or those with alternative viewpoints, and this can contribute to institutional evil.*

This is very challenging as it means that many people who think they are

ДА ЗДРАВСТВУЮТ АРТИЛЛЕРИСТЫ
И МИНОМЕТЧИКИ КРАСНОЙ АРМИИ!

Nationalism can contribute to or create many evils

good and who are not aware of doing anything wrong – much less of doing anything evil – may actually be contributing to institutional evil which causes massive harm and suffering to large numbers of people.

Lack of tolerance of dissent, lack of a willingness to challenge one's own framework or lack of a willingness to have regard for the opinions or perspectives of those outside one's own institutions, community or group may all be indications of the possible presence of institutional evil.

If a person is ignorant of the consequences of his or her actions, this does not mean that the actions are then right:

- *Those who made the bone crushing machines used to dispose of the bodies after the holocaust may not have thought the use to which the machines were put was their responsibility.*

- *Those who make and sell weapons to poor countries may not consider that the use to which the weapons will be put is their responsibility, but if one is making a weapon it is reasonable to predict that at some time it will be used and because this is a reasonable expectation the maker of the weapon and the one who sells it are partly responsible for the use to which it will be put.*

The causes of poverty, unemployment and homelessness are often complex and removed from those most effected

Peter Singer

"The visible presence of the homeless is now just another facet of American life. By the end of the Reagan years the federal government was spending $8 billion a year on housing, as compared with $32 billion at the end of the Carter administration, when homelessness was far less widespread. During these same years, however, income tax rates were falling. By then, even the very richest members of society – those earning a taxable income of more than $200,000 a year – were paying federal income tax at a rate of only 24%. Had they been taxed at 1979 rates, an extra $82 billion would have been raised – far more than was saved by cutting the housing budget. A society that prefers to cut tax rates on the very rich rather than to help the poor and the homeless has ceased to be a community in the real sense of the term." (Peter Singer, Opus 1997 ISBN 0-19-289295-9 p.33)

• Those who vote for governments that are concerned with the self-interest of their own citizens and not with those of the wider world community are partly responsible for the failure of their country to respond to the needs of the wider world.

• Those who put first their own religious group or their own family are failing to see that all human beings share a common human nature and that responsibility must extend beyond the groups to which an individual happens to belong.

One of the greatest problems in identifying institutional evil is that it can be present when no one recognizes it. The United States justice system is one of the best in the world, yet for many people the justice system is unfair and unjust and the people who contribute to the system are contributors to institutional evil. A very few lawyers recognize this and campaign for a change in the system, but most of them do not and thus they may be held to be contributors to institutional evil. In the panel below, one lawyer has set out his ideas on the key features needed to avoid institutional evil in the legal system – they seem simple requirements but, in fact, they challenge the very basis on which much of the United States legal system is based:

Reducing institutional evil in the legal area

Professor Douglas Linder of the University of Missouri/Kansas law school produced the following list of ways of reducing institutional evil in the legal system:

a) Promote tolerance through free speech. Protecting the freedom of speech of those with whom we totally disagree makes people more tolerant – and tolerant people are less inclined to develop the "us versus them" mentality that is often associated with evil.

b) Pay attention to consequences. This is much easier said than done, but a constant focus on the human consequences of decisions – a thoughtfulness – is the most important key to avoiding evil.

c) Reduce career incentives that do not take into account the effects of actions on human beings. For example, legal prosecutors should be rewarded based on how well they serve justice, not on their win-loss records. If justice is ignored then all that matters is whether a case is won or lost, not whether justice is served.

d) Arrange the legal system so that there is more contact between those who make decisions and those who are affected by these decisions. The more interaction that occurs, the greater the opportunities for empathy to develop and for the human consequences of decisions to be fully weighed. Give judges the discretion to be lenient if there are circumstances which justify leniency.

e) Facilitate the development of empathy in homes and in schools. Promote strong families and encourage new programs in schools to develop the pragmatic art of living well.

f) Choose heroes wisely. Hold up those who have served justice, not those who have achieved fame or financial success.

g) Maintain a strong belief in objective value. The central values of western civilization – mercy, truth telling, respect for parents and elders, duties to children, justice, equality, magnanimity, reverence for life should be accepted, not questioned.

THE CAUSES OF INSTITUTIONAL EVIL

1. Martha Nussbaum, Levinas and Douglas Linder all, in different ways, emphasize the dangers of any approach which helps people to identify with their own group and treat others who do not belong as "them" or "not-us". Nussbaum considers this to be the most dangerous feature of the United States after the events of September 11 – there has been a closing of ranks in the United States and a feeling that every US citizen is part of "us", US politicians and even more the armed forces are identified with "us" and no word of criticism can be tolerated against "us". Almost everyone else is "not-us" although a few outside groups which always support the US without question (such as Britain or Australia) are regarded as being part of "us" although to a restricted degree. Everyone else is regarded as "them" and their views are not taken seriously and are dismissed without being carefully considered or analyzed. The world then becomes seen in clear black and white terms – "us" is good, "them" is bad. Any measures taken against "them" becomes acceptable provided these measures are in the interests of "us".

What is lost in this approach is any compassion for or empathy with "the other". "Them", the other, becomes marginalized and their importance is denied. The root of all institutional evil lies here:

It is almost always easier to identify institutional evil in retrospect. When a person is part of the institution, many things are taken for granted that may later be seen as unacceptable.

The institutional evil of the Third Reich was clear but it was made up of millions of individual Germans who went along with a system many of them must have known was wrong. At the end of the day institutions are made up of individuals and it is individuals who are morally accountable and are responsible if they fail to stand up to the evil in which they participate.

This presents the greatest challenges – firstly to identify evil within our own institutions which we normally take for granted and secondly to then try to challenge and change these evils.

• *In South Africa, under the old apartheid regime, those with a black or coloured skin were treated as of little importance. They were different, they were "the other", so their interests could be disregarded by the well meaning and well-intentioned white community.*

• *In big business, the interests of small consumers or workers are often treated as of little importance – what matters are the shareholders, bankers, director and managers as they are part of the "us" that controls the financial system and everyone else can be exploited as they are "them".*

• *In international trade, it is the Western world that is considered to matter most (since* the institutions are controlled and funded by the Western countries) and the genuine interests of the poor countries of the world are rarely considered, leading to institutional evil on a grand scale.

- International drug companies will work to produce drugs that will cure Western diseases for people who can pay so that the companies can get a return on their investments. This means that they will not seek cures for diseases common in poor countries since the financial rewards will not be present or drugs that are developed will not help the poor of the world because the cost is too great. In the West, for instance, AIDS is held in check by the new drugs that have been developed but in Africa millions die every year at a young age and in some countries 25% of babies are born with AIDS because the drugs are too expensive. The poor of the Third World are "not us" and, therefore, governments and people of the Western world do not see any need to alter the structures to save lives.

- In international arms trade and cigarette manufacture there is no empathy for those who will be affected by the products sold to their customers – and those on whom the arms will be used or on whom the tobacco smoke will be exhaled – are regarded as "them" and not "us".

Tobacco companies market their products aggressively to the young and in third world countires where there are few controls with no regard for the suffering inflicted

- *Cosmetic companies feel free to exploit animals as animals are "not human" and, therefore, not part of the area of moral concern that "we" human beings represent.*

If failure of compassion or empathy is one of the reasons for institutional evil, the remedy lies in developing compassion and empathy. This means, from childhood, challenging those value systems which tend to minimize the importance of "the other" and to try to really take seriously both the importance, value and opinions of those who do not belong to the various groups with which people naturally identify (national, racial and religious groups, corporations, schools or colleges, families etc) This is exceptionally difficult but may be a key to overcoming institutional evil.

2. The absence of an agreed value system outside of the institution makes institutional evil particularly hard to recognize and confront. In a post-modern world, where one value system is often regarded as being as good as any other, the value system of an institution is particularly difficult to challenge. What grounds are there for suggesting that the system is wrong? In comparison to what? Unless there is general acceptance of absolute standards, which our institutions can be measured against, there seems little hope for change.

Norman Parker. The Escape

Those who resist change can claim that the values of the institution are as good as any others. Even if institutional evil can be clearly identified, it is still exceptionally difficult to address. By its nature institutional evil is the accepted norm and it seems almost impossible to overcome the power and assumptions of the institutions of which the individual forms part.

Modern art can be an aid to identifying the assumptions made about our institutions that need to be recognized and challenged. Norman Parker's painting "The Escape" raises the question of whether the prison wire – the limits that hold people within the framework of the institutions they have grown up in – are in fact self-imposed and self-created. Many do not want to escape. This was the point raised by Plato in his story of "The Cave". Combating institutional evil and all other evils requires individuals to escape from the intellectual, cultural and psychological prisons that surround them and to think through where they stand in the world and to what extent they acquiesce or accept evil which no one else sees.

John Donne expressed well the solidarity that is needed if institutional evil is to be avoided:

For Whom the Bell Tolls by John Donne (1624)

> No man is an island,
> Entire of itself.
> Each is a piece of the continent,
> A part of the main.
> If a clod be washed away by the sea,
> Europe is the less.
> As well as if a promontory were.
> As well as if a manor of thine own
> Or of thine friend's were.
>
> Each man's death diminishes me,
> For I am involved in mankind.
> Therefore, send not to know
> For whom the bell tolls;
> It tolls for thee.

QUESTIONS FOR CONSIDERATION

1. Do you consider that people who do nothing when they see an injustice taking place are morally responsible for their lack of action?

2. Do you consider that those who do not take the trouble to find out whether injustice is taking place are morally responsible for this failure?

3. If you had lived in Nazi Germany in 1936 what would you have done when Jewish or homosexual friends were taken away by the authorities? What do you think you should have done?

4. Why should anyone care when other people suffer?

5. Do you agree with Peter Singer that a society that ceases to care for those who are weak and vulnerable cannot be described as a community?

6. Do you consider there is anything wrong with companies using child labour in Third World countries in order to keep down the cost of clothing in the Western world?

CHAPTER THIRTEEN

THE GREATEST EVIL

I n this book various sources of evil have been analyzed and various
theories explained which could account for evil. Three points have
become clear, however:

*1. The freedom of human beings to choose to be selfish, self-centered and to
ignore the demands and interests of others is central to any understanding
of evil.*

*2. The human psyche is a dark and complex place and the source of many
individual evil acts lie outside of conscious control in the psyche – these are
often caused by events in childhood, repressed sexuality or a failure to come
to terms with the difficulties and failure of relationships or of death itself.*

*3. Institutional evil represents probably the most pervasive, difficult to identify
and hard to remedy evil. It dwells in nation states, in companies, in schools,
in police forces, in churches and religious groupings, in family and racial
groups and can be masked by apparently good people ignoring its reality.*

Many other factors, such as whether there is an independent force of evil, may
be debated, but these three are abundantly clear and the terrible damage they
inflict has been all too obvious over the last hundred years and, indeed, over
the whole of human history. Human beings have only recently begun to
understand the forces at work that produce evil but the three factors above
lie at the heart of many of the greatest evils and of much of the world's suffering.

Does religion, therefore, have a distinctive contribution to make to a modern understanding of evil? Many today would deny this and would say that knowledge of psychology has displaced talk of God or of the devil and would claim that the lessons of the great world religions are no longer important. This, however, may be a part of the problem. It signposts a refusal to engage deeply with different perspectives on the problem of evil – a refusal to acknowledge the possibility of the existence of God. A determination to seek naturalistic explanations for evil in fact rules out the validity of centuries of human experience and the reflections of many great thinkers of the past. If psychology can explain evil and the darkness of the human heart what it does not offer is a way for human beings to resist the temptation of evil, nor does it offer a vision of what it is to live a good life or any objective standards of goodness against which our institutions may be judged. Perhaps the contribution of world religions should not be dismissed lightly.

THE HEBREW SCRIPTURES

The greatest evil in the Hebrew Scriptures is idol worship. This is the greatest sin and the cause of much suffering. The first two of the Ten Commandments give the injunction against idolatry (see box).

Today, in any list of evils, these commandments would be seen as largely irrelevant but this is because their significance is not always recognized. The Hebrew Scriptures insist that people are the creatures of God

Central Commandments

Then God delivered... these commandments:

"I, the Lord, am your God who brought you out of the land of Egypt, the place of slavery. You shall not have other gods besides me.

You shall not carve idols for yourselves in the shape of anything in the sky above or on the earth below or in the waters beneath the earth; you shall not bow down before them or worship them. For I, the Lord, your God, am a jealous God, inflicting punishment for their father's wickedness on the children of those who hate me, down to the third and fourth generation; but bestowing mercy down to the thousandth generation on the children of those who love me and keep my commandments." (Exodus 2:1-6)

What are the gods of your organization, school, nation or family?

It can be worth writing these down in order of priority for each of the above. Gods are those things people serve or worship by centering their lives on them. They may be the God of money, of technology, of appearance, of sport, of reputation, of fitness, of fashion, of sex or many others. An organisation, or family can itself become a God. Gods cannot be criticized – so if a nation is held to be always right and if service of the nation is central, the nation may itself become a God. An example could be the state of Israel to some Jews

Jeremiah

Jeremiah prophesied in God's name against the evils of the kingdom of Israel:

"I will pronounce my sentence against them for all their wickedness in forsaking me, And in burning incense to strange gods and adoring their own handiwork" (Jeremiah 1:16)

"Roam the streets of Jerusalem, look about and observe, Search through her public places, to find even one who lives uprightly and seeks to be faithful ..." (Jeremiah 5:1)

God saw evil everywhere – yet most of the people thought that this was nonsense. They refused to see what was wrong with their society. Jeremiah prophesied that God would totally destroy Jerusalem and the people of Israel would be taken away as captives.

and that only a life lived in recognition of this is a good life. A life with any other centre would "miss the mark". Because life is a divine gift self-centered action is quite wrong, as all other people are to be respected and valued as equals. In the Hebrew Scriptures one of the signs of an evil generation is a refusal to care for the weak. The weak in Hebrew scriptural terms were the widows and orphans who had nobody to provide for them. There was equally a sacred duty to care for the stranger, for those who were "not us" as much as for the neighbour. Israel was not an insular people – they were fiercely loyal to God but they believed that their God was the creator of the whole world. This meant that other people had to be respected as well as their own.

This teaching may provide some starting points for accepted norms of behaviour in a modern world – the obligation to the weak, the poor and the oppressed seems particularly relevant in a world where the divide between rich and poor, the first world and the developing world is ever increasing. The obligation to regard the stranger as an equal member of the global society also resonates a great wisdom that it seems is often forgotten in the constant round of capitalist activity in a free market economy. The Hebrew people were commanded not to worship idols or other gods. What might these be in modern society? It could be argued that both individuals and organizations each have their own gods and they worship them by centering their lives on these gods. The language of "worshipping other gods" or idol worship is not modern day language, but if

The lamentations of Jeremiah

individuals set themselves up as authorities in themselves and refuse to recognize any absolute value system, other than when it is convenient, they as individuals become the "god" of values, deciding what is acceptable or unacceptable. If racism is deemed acceptable there is ultimately no absolute appeal against this. There is no right or wrong, only those with power who are willing to use it. Equally, if there is no measure against which the value systems of institutions can be evaluated the rules of the institution are effectively "god". Everything becomes secondary to the great god of the institution, and anything that does not serve the needs of the institution must be dispensed with. This includes the people employed by the institution who are necessarily seen as means to an end – only there to serve the needs of the institution and to be disposed

Examples of the anger Of the prophets

"There is no faithfulness or kindness or knowledge of God in the land; there is swearing, lying, killing, stealing and committing adultery; they break all bounds and murder follows murder. Therefore the land mourns and all who dwell in it languish and also the beasts of the field and the birds of the air; and even the fish of the sea are taken away." (Hosea 4:1-2)

"For three transgressions of israel and for four I will not revoke my word; but because they sell the righteous for silver and the needy for a pair of shoes – they that trample the head of the poor into the dust of the earth; and turn aside the way of the afflicted; a man and his father go into the same maiden so that my holy name is profaned ... "(Amos 2: 6 & 7) of when their usefulness expires or they become too expensive for the balance sheet to withstand.

The role of the prophets of Israel was to forcefully draw the attention of the people back to fundamental values.

The prophets came into the comfortable world that the people lived in and showed them how out of balance their lives were. They were often unpopular as they stood on the side of the weak and oppressed against the strong.

So much did kings and leaders resent the prophets that they tried to put them to death.

The prophets' role is vital as they stand on the side of what is right and are not frightened of the anger of kings or even of the mass of ordinary people. Even when they are put to death they are not fearful, as they believe their cause is just. The message of the Hebrew Scriptures may therefore offer some insights for today. Whilst the common philosophy in a post-modern world rejects absolute values it may be that a minimum commitment to values is needed which are regarded as enduring and applicable to all people for all time. If evils such as the holocaust are to be avoided in the future then each individual has to be valued as a person, and there has to be an obligation on every individual to the poor, the weak and the oppressed. This might provide starting points for an agreed set of values. It is hard for the individual to feel, in the face of evil, that they have any power, yet history has shown time and again that this is not the case. The story of human history is the story of individuals who have been prepared to stand against what is wrong, to speak out when they see injustice, to support the rights of the weak and the poor. The individual is the only person, in fact, who can do this.

The sermon on the mount

THE CHRISTIAN SCRIPTURES

Jesus said that the whole of his teaching could be summed up in two commandments:

1. You shall love the Lord your God with all your heart, mind and soul, and

2. You shall love your neighbour as yourself.

These two commandments summed up the whole of the Jewish Law and the prophets. These commandments are so well known that today many do not understand how radical they are, yet Jesus himself spelt out their consequences on more than one occasion. First of all he challenged the accepted wisdom that loyalty to family was the highest duty. He specifically rejected his own brothers and sisters and members of his family and said that his followers would often face the anger of their own families and that they should not even pause to bury their dead father! He did this at a time when

Jesus purifies the temple

Israel was held together by loyalty to family and to tribe and he made clear that his followers were bound together by new ties which transcended the local communities to which they happened to belong.

More than this, however, Jesus continually challenged his own society by rejecting the "insider/outsider" distinctions that they imposed. The Jewish community of Jesus' time was in many ways insular. Specifically they rejected:

1. *Gentiles – all those who were not born Jewish. They saw themselves as superior to these gentiles and in many ways looked down on them.*

2. *Romans – the Romans were the last in a long line of foreigners who had conquered their country and they were bitterly resented by the Jews. The Romans were obvious by their military presence and even more by the taxation they levied. They had even built a fortress in one corner of the Holy Temple in Jerusalem. They were despised by the Jews and a radical set of Jews, the Zealots, waged a small scale guerrilla war against the Romans.*

3. *The Samaritans – many religious groups hate those who are closest to them more than those who are further away. Thus Catholics and Protestants frequently are at enmity, Orthodox and Reformed Jews not only dislike but sometimes despise each other and the differences between Sunni and Shia Muslims lead to the communities barely mixing and sometimes being at war.*

In all such cases memories are long and recollections of the wrongs done by the "other" group are strong. In the time of Jesus the Samaritans were Jews who had remained behind during the time of the Babylonian captivity. They were considered to have betrayed true Judaism and were despised and rejected by all good, orthodox, mainstream Jewish opinion.

Jesus, however, accepted none of these distinctions – indeed the Gospels record quite the opposite. He went out of his way to show that faith in God and goodness did not depend on belonging to a particular race or institution. For instance:

1. *Jesus rejected the male, patriarchal society of his time by mixing freely with women, both married and non-married. It was women who were with him when he died and a woman who was first to come to his tomb after his death.*

2. *He did not condemn (as the Jewish law required) a woman actually taken in the act of adultery.*

3. *Normally women with periods were considered ritually unclean yet when a woman who had a permanent period quietly touched the hem of Jesus' cloak he did not condemn her but rather affirmed her femininity and cured her.*

4. *Jesus cured a Roman centurion's servant and said that he found greater faith in this Roman centurion than in the whole of the people of Israel.*

5. *He did not condemn paying taxes to the occupying Roman authorities.*

6. *The parable of the Good Samaritan is, perhaps, one of the strongest statements of Jesus' position. He told the story of a man who was robbed and left lying beside the road. The man had no money and was badly injured and close to death. A priest came along and saw the injured man but he had appointments to keep and looking after the man would have meant that he could not take a service to which he was travelling and so he left the injured man lying there and passed on his way. Then a scholar, someone trained in the Jewish Law, came by and also saw the injured man but, again, he had things to do so he ignored the injured man and passed on his way. Then along came a despised Samaritan and it was this man who stopped, bound up the wounds of the injured man, carried him on his own*

donkey to the next town, took him to an
inn and paid for him to be cared for and
looked after. Jesus' points are very clear –

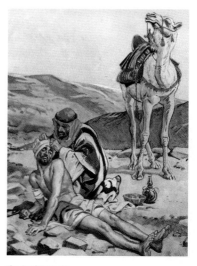

a. the "insider/outsider" distinction
   which lies at the root of institutional
   evil must be rejected,

b. every person has a responsibility to
   combat evil and, no matter who the
   person is, if they fail to combat evil
   they are in the wrong and

c. goodness is to be found amongst
   those who actively commit themselves
   to caring for others not in those who
   talk about it and do not act.

The Good Samaritan

7. The most surprising and uncomfortable message of Jesus on evil comes in
   his teaching on the separation of those who are good and those who are evil
   and their different treatment after death. This teaching is clear and
   unambiguous and likely to be very disturbing for many who consider
   themselves to be "good" Christians. Jesus says that at the final judgment
   the good will go to heaven and those who are evil will go to hell but the
   separation will be made not on what people have said in church or on what
   they have said they have believed but on how they have acted:

   • The good are those who cared for the sick, visited those in prison, given
     food and water to those who had nothing to eat or drink. All these
     people, whether or not they believed in God or in Jesus, would be
     considered to have been doing these services as if they were done
     directly to Jesus himself. In other words, when someone cares for and
     helps those in need, this is equivalent to directly helping Jesus himself.
     This, however, is not the surprising part.

   • The challenging teaching is that those who do nothing, those who may
     think themselves good, go to church each week and participate in their
     religious groupings will be condemned as evil BECAUSE THEY FAILED TO
     ACT. The failure to act is itself an evil act. This is precisely what many

modern philosophers have said and, again, reflects the crucial importance of institutional evil. Simply by conforming to one's group, by obeying the ethical system of the nation or community within which one lives a person does not become good. Certainly such a person may consider themselves to be good but in fact they may well be evil because they have acquiesced in an evil system.

Being part of a community is a good thing. Human beings are social animals and find their meaning and their roles in life as part of communities. However it is when the values of the community are adopted unthinkingly, unquestioningly that the danger of evil arises. It is then that the power of those who control society is at its strongest (exercised often through the media) and if post-modernism is accepted there is no longer any ground for preferring one society's value systems to that of another. Signs of this power in use include when the community's values become so strong that it persecutes those who challenge it. It is then that the community is most suspect and most to be feared. It is also when it most needs to be challenged.

Tolstoy's novel *Resurrection*

In Tolstoy's novel *Resurrection* the story is told of a young man who goes to visit his aunt's house in the country and falls in love with a young orphan girl who is staying in the house. Although the couple are young they are sure of their love and make love. He leaves to go to the army and soon forgets her. She, however, finds that she is pregnant. The aunts throw her out of the house and she has nowhere to go and no money. She is befriended by a wealthy man and supported (in return for sex). So it continues but soon her looks begin to fade and by the time she is 26 she is a common prostitute, looking old and terrible. She is arrested by the police and put on trial.

One of the magistrates is the young boy who made love to her, although he is now a very respectable and wealthy young man. He recognizes the girl in spite of her terrible change of appearance. He realizes that it is his action that is responsible for her present plight. He does everything he can to have her acquitted but she is sentenced to be sent to Siberia. The novel tells the story of how he does everything in his power to overcome the evil effects of his actions. The girl does not ask for anything but it is his guilt that drives him to act. He has been a part of a system that has caused evil and he challenges the system – although no one within the system can understand why he should care so much. He, after all, is comfortable and secure.

THE MODERN WORLD

The modern world is incredibly complex:

- *Even nation states have fairly limited power when compared with multinational corporations which often have a larger turnover than many countries.*

- *Each country has to trade with others around the world and is not allowed to make its own decisions about the way its affairs are conducted – international trade is regulated by international bodies. As an example, Australia could not prevent the import of Canadian salmon which threatened the Tasmania salmon industry because the GATT (General Agreement on Tariffs and Trade) prohibited this.*

- *The power of the media grows ever larger with organizations like News Corp (controlled by the Murdoch family) controlling television stations, magazines and newspapers around the world. These media organizations can effectively censor views they disapprove of (for instance News Corp refused to publish the memoirs of Chris Patton, the former Governor-General of Hong Kong, because the Chinese government put pressure on them not to publish as they thought the memoirs would embarass them).*

- *On the Internet the major search engines, almost all of which are American, censor various matters that are considered not to be in the interests of the United States.*

- *The real reasons behind many of the conflicts in the modern world are almost impossible to determine – for instance there has been much speculation that the real reason behind the Allied invasion of Afghanistan was due to the wish to establish an oil pipeline that the previous government had refused to accept.*

It is hard to understand all the effects that actions have and the individual seems to be increasingly powerless. Given this, how is it possible to identify evil still less to make a stand against it? The Hebrew and Christian Scriptures give two clear answers.

1. **Human beings need to live their lives responsible to a transcendent ultimate which some call God. The existence of this ultimate being**

provides a sense of personal responsibility which goes beyond the nation, community, corporation, school or even family in which a person lives and which may challenge the values accepted in the community. The primary responsibility is to this transcendent "Other" and it is this responsibility that matters more than anything else. Only this enables institutional evil and evil in society to be effectively questioned. These ideas are further developed in *Being Human* by Peter Vardy published by DLT in 2003

2. The neighbour is everyone – no matter what the colour of their skin, their beliefs or where they live – and there is a duty of love to every other person as great as the duty of love to one's own family. This seems an impossible ideal but it is the ideal that all the great religious leaders point towards.

Today, however, another factor needs to be added. The world is so complex that one has to seek, to probe and understand the consequences of actions and to be willing to challenge the assumptions of one's own community. If post-modernism is accepted then, of course, there is no intellectual basis for this challenge as there is no ultimate right or wrong. However even if post-modern is rejected, then to challenge one's community demands a high level of learning and engagement with the world in order to understand its complexity. Life may well have to be lived not by a simple set of rules but by wrestling with complexity and ambiguity to seek the good when no one path may seem right.

Evil can only be successfully resisted if ordinary people are willing to say "NO" to participating in it. Of course, there are individuals who, by themselves, do evil, but these are isolated instances and often can be explained in psychological terms. This is not to excuse the evil that individuals do, but at least some of the reasons and contributory factors can now be understood. With help from psychologists and psychotherapists, these people can be helped to recognize the factors that have led them to act as they do. In spite of this, of course, there will still be some individuals who simply choose to do evil as they place self as the center of their own lives and have no regard for anyone else. However, although the major evils in today's world may be initiated by individuals, they depend on the willingness of ordinary people to participate in the evil or at least not to challenge it.

For an individual to stand against evil is exceptionally difficult as it will often mean being willing to lose one's friends and job, to be excluded from one's social community, to be mocked and be the object of ridicule, to have one's reputation destroyed by taking a stand on an issue of principle which everyone else may consider to be unreasonable. "Everyone else", including family and friends, will tend to tell the person who takes such a stand that they should conform, that they should "go along with the system" and "not rock the boat". They will be told that, if they take a stand, then their family will be affected and as their highest responsibility is to their family, the family's interests should be put first. The point about (1) above is that it rejects this claim and holds that there is a higher responsibility – to the transcendent other many call God. Most people, of course, do not accept this, which is why evil can so easily triumph in the modern world.

Ludwig Wittgenstein said that he was a man of power – the power being to have control over himself. Few of us have this. Most go along with the group, with our families or with our communites. Really to have power over oneself can take a lifetime of effort and great commitment and dedication as well as a willingness to sacrifice one's own selfish interests.

It is fair to say that the greatest ally of the forces of evil is conformity and, therefore, that the central evil is conformity. Conformity lulls people into a sense of security, into the feeling that all that is required is to comply with the standard of the community in which they live. It was this that allowed the evil of Nazi Germany, the evils of Stalin's Russia or of Rwanda, the evils of Pol Pot's regime in Cambodia or the evil of corporate greed in the modern day world to survive and prosper. The great Hebrew prophets recognized this and stood alone on the side of God against their own community, but it is a hard and lonely position. Elijah, one of the greatest prophets, recognized this when he was alone in the desert with many of his fellow prophets having been killed. He says to God:

"I have been most zealous for the LORD, the God of hosts, but the Israelites have forsaken your covenant, torn down your altars, and put your prophets to the sword. I alone am left, and they seek to take my life." (1 Kings 19:10)

The same picture of a lonely willingness to stand on the side of the good against the forces of evil applied in Jesus' time and also today. Few are willing to pay the price to make such a stand. Jesus was crucified – he was desert-

Jesus on the cross dies alone, standing outside the communites which condemned him, having lived a life dedicated to God. By his death, he overcome death and also gave the ultimate picture of a life lived for Truth, Goodness and Love no matter what the cost

ed by his friends, denied three times by his closest friend and he stood alone in front of his accusers. Few people today would have had the courage to endure what he did when it would have been so easy for him to compromise and to go free. The leaders of the institutions of his day (the Romans and the Temple authorities) simply wanted life to continue in a way that enabled people to live together. They did not want trouble.

Jesus resisted evil by refusing to give in to it. He showed the power of goodness through weakness by refusing to let his life be compromised by those forces that sought to take over his teaching. He rejected force or even seeking to persuade people to follow him by public displays of miracles – instead he brought forgiveness and the possibility of a new start to people from every walk of life from tax collectors to priests and prostitutes. He lived by the law of love and applied it no matter what the status of the person. He called his followers to put God and love first no matter what the personal cost and said that the few who would be willing to take this hard, lonely path of living a life of goodness would face persecution and possibly death. The centuries since have provided abundant evidence that he was right

It is one thing to talk of the need to stand on the side of the good, the just and the true, responsible to a transcendent reality, against the institutional evil of the world, but this still leaves open the issue as to how an individual can decide on the difference between good and evil in the complex world in which we live. These issues are explored in a companion book in this series called *The Thinker's guide to Ethics*.

In Harry Potter the two key characters apart from Harry himself are Professor Dumbledore and Lord Voldermort. One lives for others and the other lives for self. Lord Vodermort, ever since he was merely Tom Riddle and a student of

Hogwarts, put his own selfish interests first. Dumbledore does not think of his own interests. The same applies in the *Lord of the Rings* where Gandalf is pitted against Sauron and Saruman. Again the contrast is between a life lived for others and a life lived for self. Evil is a choice – but it then becomes a way of life that affects the whole personality. It is possible to turn one's back on past choices but it is exceptionally difficult – to a large extent we are made by the choices we have made but hope always remains as forgiveness and a new start are always possible, even at the last moment.

At the end of the day evil is not simply an academic problem, it represents a choice affecting each individual. Every day people face a choice: to go along with a comfortable life or to stand up for Goodness, Truth and Justice no matter what the consequences may be. However uncomfortable and challenging it may seem, this remains a real possibility. Whether, of course, we are individually willing to pay the price of standing against evil is another matter – this is a decision that each of us has to make for ourselves. However, if we refuse to stand up then we ourselves may become part of the evil that dominates so much of our world.

A Poem

Once to every man and nation, Comes the moment to decide,

In the strife of truth with false-hood, For the good or evil side;

Some great cause, some great decision, Offering each the bloom or blight,

And the choice goes by forever, 'Twixt that darkness and that light.

Then to side with truth is noble, When we share her wretched crust,

Ere her cause bring fame and profit, And 'tis prosperous to be just;

Then it is the brave man chooses, While the coward stands aside,

Till the multitude make virtue, of the faith they had denied.

Though the cause of evil prosper, Yet the truth alone is strong:

Though her portion be the scaffold, And upon the throne be wrong,

Yet that scaffold sways the future, and, behind the dim unknown,

Standeth God within the shadow, keeping watch above his own.

James Russell Lowell (1819-1891)